Gifts from the Spirit

Gifts from the Spirit

Reflections on the Diaries and Letters
of Anne Morrow Lindbergh

Kim Jocelyn Dickson

A CROSSROAD CARLISLE BOOK
THE CROSSROAD PUBLISHING COMPANY
NEW YORK ◆ BERKELEY

The Crossroad Publishing Company
481 Eighth Avenue, New York, NY 10001

Printed in the United States of America

Library of Congress Cataloging-in-Publication Data

Dickson, Kim Jocelyn.
  Gifts from the spirit : reflections on the diaries and letters of Anne Morrow Lindbergh / Kim Jocelyn Dickson.
      p. cm.
  "A Crossroad Carlisle book."
  ISBN 0-8245-2010-6
    1. Lindbergh, Anne Morrow, 1906—Criticism and interpretation. 2.Lindbergh, Anne Morrow, 1906—Diaries. 3. Air pilots—United States--Diaries. 4. Life. 5. Feminist spirituality. I. Lindbergh, Anne Morrow, 1906- Diaries Selections. II. Title.
TL540.L49 D53 2002
818'.5'209--dc21

                                                         2002004483

1 2 3 4 5 6 7 8 9 10   08 07 06 05 04 03 02

Acknowledgement is gratefully given to Harcourt Inc. for permission to reprint excerpts from the following works by Anne Morrow Lindbergh:

  *Bring Me a Unicorn: Diaries and Letters of Anne Morrow Lindbergh
      1922-1928* © 1972
  *Hour of Gold, Hour of Lead: Diaries of Anne Morrow Lindbergh,
      1929-1932* © 1973
  *Locked Rooms and Open Doors: Diaries and Letters of Anne Morrow
      Lindbergh, 1933-1935* ©1974
  *The Flower and the Nettle: Diaries and Letter of Anne Morrow Lindbergh,
      1936-1939* © 1976
  *War Within And Without: Diaries and Letters of Anne Morrow Lindbergh,
      1939-1944* © 1980

The rest of the picture—the picture that emerged as I read her published diaries and letters—is that of a woman who was alienated from herself, who struggled to understand herself, her relationships, and her place in the world. I saw a woman who had *not* arrived, but was on a journey—a journey toward self-awareness.

Anne's body of literary work follows the same theme: The journey of spiritual awareness—of coming home to yourself. Whether it's her poetry, her prose, or her personal writings in her diaries and letters, she takes her reader by the hand, and graciously, companionably, points the way: *Take the inner road*, she says. *The answers are inside you.*

— *from the Introduction*

Contents

My Introduction to Anne   ix

A Word About Anne   xv

Children Aren't Born to Live Their Parents' Lives   3

Finding Nourishment for the Soul in Nature   6

Struggling to Embrace Her Own True Feelings   10

The Poet, the Pilot, and their Passion   12

The Key to Making Her Life Count   18

The Hope of Spring in Her Spirit   21

The Heart Behind the Facade   24

Life is Found in the Shadow of Death   27

The Way Life Should Be   31

What Is This Thing That Is Presence and Yet
Not Presence?   37

Embracing Grief as a Path to Peace   43

The Exhilaration of Being Yourself   47

Moments of Heightened Awareness   51

Looking for Her True Home   55

The Flow of Eternal Life   59

Red Shoes and the Search for Self   64

Reading to Know You're Not Alone   ⊗   68

Comfort for the Body is Comfort for the Spirit   ⊗   72

Love and the Stream of Compassion   ⊗   76

Friendship for Life   ⊗   80

Trust Your Apathy   ⊗   86

It's What You Don't Know About Yourself
That Can Hurt You   ⊗   90

Writing Through the Pit of Fear   ⊗   93

Growth Underground   ⊗   98

The Spiritual Value of Possessions   ⊗   102

Our Legacy to Our Children   ⊗   106

A Fertile Garden   ⊗   111

The Smallest Gesture Reveals the Person   ⊗   116

Hope for Old Age   ⊗   120

How Intimacy is Possible   ⊗   124

Space to Breathe   ⊗   128

Leap of Faith Inward   ⊗   133

Doorway to the Divine   ⊗   138

All Vulnerability and Sweetness   ⊗   142

The Soul of a Marriage   ∞   145

The God Has Left the Temple   ∞   151

The Must of Mutuality in a Relationship   ∞   157

The Heart is Slow to Learn   ∞   160

Lessons From the Journey   ∞   164

Anne's Legacy: The Journey Not the Arrival   ∞   169

BIBLIOGRAPHY   ∞   173

NOTES   ∞   175

ACKNOWLEDGMENTS   ∞   178

ABOUT THE AUTHOR   ∞   181

My Introduction to Anne

"When one finds a person who has the same thought as yours you cry out for joy, you go and shake him by the hand. Your heart leaps as though you were walking in a street in a foreign land and you heard your own language spoken, or your name in a room full of strangers."

⟿ WAR WITHIN AND WITHOUT, p.33

A picture of a young Anne Morrow Lindbergh sits on my desk. I clipped it from a second-hand bookstore copy of *Hour of Gold, Hour of Lead* and put it in a brass frame that once belonged to my grandmother. The picture of Anne's sad face, photographed shortly after the kidnapping and murder of her baby boy, has been a companion for years. It sat on my desk when I lived in Princeton, New Jersey, and it is here on my desk in Southern California, where I live now, right next to a photograph of my grandmother.

It was my grandmother's copy of *Gift From the Sea* that introduced me to Anne Morrow Lindbergh. This first edition teal-and-white volume rested untouched on a bookshelf at my parents' home for years after my grandmother's death when I was ten. During my teenage years I spent hours talking to my friends on the phone that hung on the wall next to this bookcase. I gazed at the binding of this book nearly every evening as I chatted, connecting to my friends, the world outside my family. Sometimes I even picked it up and looked at it, mildly curious about the woman married to the man for whom my high school was named. But I was not curious enough to read it. Not then anyway.

It wasn't until my twenties, when I was home on vacation from graduate school at Princeton Seminary and preoccupied about my vocational future and a man in my life, that I pulled the book out to read. I was absorbed immediately. Maybe enchanted was more like it. It wasn't just what she said—which spoke right to me—it was the way she said it. There was beauty in the way she used words. As I read on I was moved further.

Sparingly etched in blue ink throughout the book were underlines and an occasional exclamation mark: "The problem is not merely one of *Woman and Career, Woman and the Home, Woman and Independence*. It is more basically: how to remain whole in the midst of the distractions of life; how to remain balanced, no matter what centrifugal forces tend to pull one off center; how to remain strong..."[1] and "Woman must be the pioneer in this turning inward for strength..."[2] and "...women need solitude to find the true essence of themselves..."[3]

The markings were in my grandmother's handwriting. It had been more than twenty years since her eyes and hand had swept across these same pages, but at that moment I felt she was with me. Anne Morrow Lindbergh's words became a bridge for me, linking me to this woman I had loved so much and lost.

Discovering who my grandmother was through Anne's words was important to me because, in some way, that seemed to tell me more about who I was too. It was reassuring to know that the grandmother who had meant so much to me when I was small thought about her inner life. Maybe this was why I'd felt so connected to her as a child.

When you find a person *who has the same thought as yours*, you want to get to know her better. My grandmother was gone, but there was much more I would learn about Anne Morrow Lindbergh.

After reading *Gift From the Sea*, I searched for anything and everything I could find by or about her. Most of Anne's books were available at the Princeton public library, fortunately; they were nearly impossible to own, though, because nearly everything but *Gift From the Sea* and her one book of poetry, *The Unicorn*, were out of print. I became well acquainted with second-hand bookstores, and occasionally was lucky enough to find one of her books. Then the man I married conducted an all-out nationwide search—in the days before the Internet existed, mind you—and, amazingly, unearthed every hardcover volume I didn't already own, surprising me with them for a wedding present. My collection was complete.

The dearth of availability was a mystery to me. While *Gift From the Sea* continued to sell millions all over the world and had become an inspirational classic, what about the rest of her work? Why was it out of print? And why was practically nothing written about her?

I discovered Anne Morrow Lindbergh's work when I was a seminary student, struggling to learn more about the meaning of life and God—and myself. Privileged to be attending one of the best theological schools in the country, I studied with professors who were world-renowned and read widely in fields as diverse as psychology, philosophy, education, theology, Biblical studies, women's studies, and history. But what I kept coming back to, what I really wanted to read, was more of Anne, for her work touched not only my mind, but my heart, too.

I was fascinated by the life she led. As a major twentieth-century figure married to an American icon, she was both a player in and witness to some of the most important historical events of her time. But what was even more remarkable than that, to me, was her inner life. Here was a woman who, in the eyes of the outside world, seemed to have it all. Raised with all the advantages her wealthy parents could give her, Ivy League educated, married to the most popular man in the world, she was talented and successful in her own right and became a best-selling author. But this wasn't the whole picture.

The rest of the picture—the picture that emerged as I read her published diaries and letters—is that of a woman who was alienated from herself, who struggled to understand herself, her relationships, and her place in the world. I saw a woman who had *not* arrived, but was on a journey—a journey toward self-awareness.

Anne's body of literary work follows the same theme: The journey of spiritual awareness—of coming home to yourself. Whether it's her poetry, her prose, or her personal writings in her diaries and letters, she takes her reader by the hand, and graciously, companionably, points the way: *Take the inner road*, she says. *The answers are inside you.*

My Post-It note-marked, scribbled in, underlined, and highlighted five volumes of Anne's diaries and letters are scattered here on my desk today, right alongside my pictures of Anne and my grandmother. *Bring Me a Unicorn*; *Hour of Gold, Hour of Lead*; *Locked Rooms and Open Doors*; *The Flower and the Nettle*; and *War Within and Without*. These dog-eared, slightly yellowed, tattered book jacket copies were second-hand to begin with, but they are treasures to me nonetheless, for what they meant to me as a young woman who was on the threshold of self-discovery and what they mean to me still.

Coming across Anne in these books was like meeting someone who spoke the same language I did. Her reflections resonated deep inside me: *Yes. I know just what you mean.* When I read Anne's diaries and letters I felt less alone. Here was someone who struggled with the same things I struggled with, who put into words things I felt but could not articulate, who reminded me of some knowledge dormant inside me: that the things I long for are already within me. And who, by her example, gave me courage to get on with my own inner journey.

And so I did, and I'd like to share some of it with you. The passages you will read from Anne's diaries and letters are thoughts of hers that I've returned to again and again over the past twenty years. These are the reflections and observations that leapt out at me, that something inside me said *yes* to. I wasn't always conscious of why these thoughts seemed so true during my earliest readings. But as the years have gone by and I have understood more about myself, I understand more about her, too. The truth that I apprehended only dimly as a young woman has become clearer with time and self-awareness.

And so I offer one woman's take on Anne Morrow Lindbergh—who she was and what her legacy is. I hope that in my personal reflections on Anne's life and words and wisdom, you too may hear your own language spoken. Or your name in a room full of strangers.

A Word About Anne

Born in 1906 in Englewood, New Jersey, Anne Spencer Morrow was the second child in a family of three daughters and a son, a family she would describe some sixty years later as warm, close-knit, and protective.

Dwight and Elizabeth Cutter Morrow, her parents, were both born to modest circumstances, educated at prestigious Eastern schools, and brimming with energy and ambition. They led a middle class life in Englewood through their early-married years and were quite active in their small community. Dwight eventually became a partner with J.P. Morgan and Company in New York, propelling them into another stratosphere.

The Morrows' newly acquired wealth enabled them to move in circles of privilege and power. The family traveled extensively, accompanied by trunks of books and itineraries that included visits to museums, cathedrals, and other historical points of interest, as well as to the homes of leaders in European commerce and government. Morrow's success also meant private school education and Ivy League colleges for all four children, the purchase of a large apartment in New York City, a home on North Haven Island off the coast of Maine, and, later, a new address in Englewood called Next Day Hill, a large and lavish estate.

Anne grew up in a world of privilege to be sure. But with that privilege came great expectations. Anne's parents had lived the American dream. From modest circumstances they had, through hard work, talent, and good fortune, aspired to achieve and succeeded. Ironically though, the emotional undercurrent that ran through the family was not quite so rosy.

While Anne's childhood may have appeared charmed and nearly perfect, there was a dark side. Dwight and Elizabeth no doubt intended nothing but good toward their children, but their own conflicts and tensions permeated the family atmosphere. Their values, borne of self-restrained Calvinism, conflicted with their windfall of extreme wealth. Always socially conscious and active, they would both expend enormous energy toward the public good, increasingly so after becoming wealthy. Anne's reaction was ambivalent; she was incredibly proud of her parents and their achievements yet she felt a bit awed and sidelined. She knew she could never keep up with them.

But this was what was expected. Along with their strong moral code and sense of social responsibility, the Morrows highly valued education and achievement. Immersed in an atmosphere that provided the stimulation for all these things, and quite intelligent and gifted herself, Anne felt herself to be perpetually in her family's wake. As a young woman she wrote in her diary:

"I think one of us will die. It won't be me. It ought to be—I am the complete loss in our family. But the useless people never die!"[4] This statement revealed not only Anne's prescience—her older sister Elisabeth *would* die young—but also the way she saw herself. Shy, sensitive, and introspective, she held herself up to her parents' standards and found herself wanting. Her sense of being left behind was exacerbated by the fact that Elisabeth, whom Anne perceived to be more beautiful, popular, vivacious, quick-witted and charming than she, was more like her parents.

In a household of highly energetic extroverts, an atmosphere that Anne described as "nervous," Anne found limited support for her emerging sense of self. As the child of parents who were busy expending a great deal of energy justifying themselves, in avoidance, perhaps, of some deeply buried insecurities and fears of their own, the acutely reflective and introverted Anne felt unseen and, despite appearances to the contrary—emotionally estranged from her family.

Underneath her shy exterior, Anne possessed a fierce desire to find her own way. The longing would be the theme woven through all of her writing both published and private. And it would emerge dramatically in one of her most life-shaping decisions: her marriage.

Anne was ensconced in the Smith College library focused on her own literary aspirations and working on a paper on Erasmus—one of her father's favorite figures—when Charles A. Lindbergh and *The Spirit of St. Louis* touched down at Le Bourget Field in Paris in May of 1927. The ensuing tide of public adulation that swept over Lindbergh escaped Anne. Lindbergh, as the first man to fly the Atlantic solo, was catapulted to hero status. He seemed to be everything America wanted to believe about itself: he was young, strikingly attractive, dignified, courageous, and independent. Popular culture was soon swept up in a love affair with Lindbergh, which may explain why Anne was oblivious.

Virtually untouched by the pulls of the youth culture of the Roaring Twenties, Anne's world was her parents' world. What she knew was literature, art, music, and the refined people who appreciated it all. What she didn't know then was how much she longed to venture beyond. Her first published volume of diaries and letters, *Bring Me a Unicorn*, chronicles the beginning of her journey out.

The disparate worlds of Anne and Charles met when her father, then U.S. ambassador to Mexico, invited Lindbergh to spend Christmas with the Morrow family at the embassy in Mexico City as part of a good-will mission. The subsequent courtship and marriage of the two proved to be as cataclysmic for Anne as it was for the public who venerated their hero.

Enchanted with Charles's world of action, and hungry for life beyond what she had known, the newlywed Anne embraced flying. The first years of their marriage were marked by the romance and adventure of extended trips in which the two pioneered air routes all over the world. Anne learned to pilot a plane, became skilled in radio communication, and adjusted to the rigors of camping and surviving in remote, uninhabited parts of the globe.

Adopting her husband's world, however, meant letting go of her own for a time. Alongside Charles's life of action and purpose, her literary interests struck her as pale and insignificant. During this period she gave up writing virtually anything except letters to her family. She even abandoned her diary, to which she'd long been faithful.

It took a tragedy to draw her back. *Hour of Gold, Hour of Lead*, the second and perhaps best known of Anne's published diaries and letters, covers the glory of those early flying days as well as the subsequent horror when her first child, Charles A. Lindbergh, Jr., was tragically kidnapped and murdered. To cope with her loss, Anne returned to the tool that had always put her in touch with her essential self: her writing. The diary entries of this period are some of the most evocative, expressive reflections ever written on grief and loss.

The next phase of Anne's life, portrayed in *Locked Room and Open Doors*, is full of poignancy. Inwardly, she continued to grieve the loss of her son and struggled against the circumstances of her life. The fame that had surrounded the Lindberghs from the beginning and at first brought annoyance and inconvenience, now became increasingly oppressive. From the moment the press discovered the courtship of Anne and Charles, the union of these intensely private people took on a life of its own in the public domain. Ironically, these two, each of whom had a high need to flee the boundaries of their families of origin, ran up against constrictions of another kind. They were, before the Kennedy era, unquestionably America's royalty. Public hunger for information and photographs of them was intense and they were relentlessly pursued. The Lindberghs, always resentful of the intrusion of journalists, blamed the blaze of publicity surrounding them for the death of their son. Outwardly, Anne coped by continuing the exploratory flights with her husband. When she took to the air for remote parts of the world, she hoped to escape the unyielding publicity—and the crushing weight of her loss. When they returned to earth it was to live with Anne's widowed mother. They sought to support her— she'd lost both her husband and daughter Elisabeth in a short space of time—as well as find the protection for their family they felt only her highly secure estate could provide. But going back home only inflamed Anne's angst.

During this time she channeled her creative energy into her first book, *North to the Orient*. The story of the Lindberghs' first air trip together was a milestone for Anne, not only because it was critically and popularly well received, but because it allayed many of her doubts about her ability to write.

Anne's joy in the birth of her second son, Jon, and in the publication of her first book was not without a shadow, though. Publicity intensified around them as the man accused of kidnapping and murdering their son was brought to trial. When they received letters threatening their second son, the Lindberghs decided they could not live normal lives in America, and they sailed for Europe.

Settling into a rambling manor in the English countryside and later into a primitive castle on an island off the coast of Brittany, Anne found the peace, privacy, and domestic happiness she craved. Relieved of the burden she'd felt living under her mother's roof, she reveled in the quiet life that nourished her family and her own creativity. During this time she gave birth to her third son, Land, and wrote and published *Listen! the Wind*, the second book to recount a flying trip with her husband. Even more enthusiastically received than her first, Anne's deepening as a writer was evident.

Anne's European years, chronicled in *The Flower and the Nettle*, were the backdrop for her personal renewal and growing sense of self. From her first years with Charles when she had thrown off her own world of writing as inconsequential and embraced his world of action as all-important, to the publication of her second, critically acclaimed book, she had begun a quiet, but tortured, inner evolution. Her suffering because of the death of her son played no small part in this. Anne was forced to find the part of herself that was essential simply to go on. For her that meant writing.

She began to come into her own during her European years. In reclaiming neglected parts of herself and integrating the ways in which her life with Charles had expanded her personality, Anne experienced one of the happiest periods of her life. But her tranquility was not to last.

Anne's diaries and letters from this period are fascinating, not only because of her personal journey of self-renewal, but because they offer a rare glimpse into the elite private and government circles of the turbulent period of pre-war Europe. Charles was a private citizen, but because of his heroic stature and aviation expertise he and Anne were frequent guests of Europe's upper echelon that included royalty and government leaders. When at the request of the U.S. Embassy in Berlin Charles was asked to visit Germany to assess its pre-war airpower, rumors accusing him of Nazi sympathies began to circulate in the United States. The Lindberghs' involvement in the conflicts of the war years opened yet another painful chapter in Anne's life.

Anne returned to America with Charles and her two sons shortly before the war broke out in Europe in 1939. As a pacifist she actively supported her husband's efforts to prevent the United States from entering the war in Europe. Anne's own abhorrence of war seasoned with Charles's views and her loyalty to him resulted in an attempt to explain her position in a lengthy essay published as a small book: *The Wave of the Future*. The reaction was fierce. She was severely criticized as naive and as advocating passive acceptance of totalitarianism, all of which added to her growing sense of isolation. Charles's America First endeavors were highly unpopular with Anne's Eastern intellectual family and friends and the couple was shunned by many. Never had Anne felt so torn between her past and the man she'd chosen. Caught between her conflicting loyalties, she once again turned to writing. *War Within and Without* contains the diaries and letters that recount this difficult time.

Then Anne met a man who would have a lasting impact on her. Anne's publisher, Harcourt Brace, had asked the French writer and pilot, Antoine de Saint-Exupéry to write a forward for the French edition of Anne's book *Listen! the Wind*. Not knowing her and expecting a "potboiler," he agreed to do a one-page preface, but upon reading the book he was so moved that he wrote nine. He also wanted to meet her. After reading his analysis, Anne was stunned by what he saw of her and by the importance he ascribed to her book. For the first time in her life she felt that someone truly saw who she was. That he grasped her essence—not as her parent's daughter or her husbands' wife or the image the world had of her—but as the gifted woman she was in her own right, whose power came from her core vulnerability and anguish. "There is a little girl who runs more slowly than the others...[who fears she] will be forgotten and left alone in the world."[5] Saint-Exupéry had read the emotional reality behind Anne's words as no one had before. Their face-to-face meeting was just as powerful for her. They connected immediately. Despite the awkwardness of their language differences, their conversation was filled with understanding. They spoke the same language—the language of people in touch with their inner worlds.

The meeting emboldened Anne to attempt fiction for the first time. *The Steep Ascent* was a fictionalized account of an event that happened when Charles and Anne flew over the Swiss Alps. This story of a near-death flying experience shared by a husband and wife became a powerful allegory for communicating her own understanding of life, death, and spiritual rebirth. She admitted in her diary that "all that she knew" went into the book, and she "sent it out" as you would a letter—to Saint-Exupéry, the one person she was sure would understand it. Her philosophy of life is crystallized here. Anne's experience of spiritual descent into hell with the tragic loss of her son and her slow but painful subsequent rebirth to life unconsciously permeates every page. While ultimately life affirming, Anne shows that death is part of the process of life that can't be denied or ignored. Embracing loss is what ultimately frees us to live fully and richly. Sadly, Saint-Exupéry was killed in a reconnaissance flight over France during the war and didn't live to read the book. But the impact of their connection would affect Anne always.

Had Saint-Exupéry lived to read Anne's published diaries and letters which end at the close of the war, he would have found there the same vulnerability and genius that he discovered in her early travel book. When one reads them one realizes Anne's life itself was the source of all she wrote. The chronicles of this artist, wife, and mother of five children are the wellspring of her literary work, revealing the journey of a woman in search of her deepest self—aspiring to love, share her gifts, and find her place in the world.

The origins of the book Anne would write almost ten years after the end of the war that would secure her place in publishing history is also found in these volumes. Her jewels of wisdom, polished so beautifully and set off to perfection in *Gift From the Sea*, are right there in *Bring Me a Unicorn; Hour of Gold, Hour of Lead; Locked Rooms and Open Doors; The Flower and the Nettle;* and *War Within and Without*—not as polished or perfect or shiny, but maybe even more valuable because of it.

Strewn throughout Anne's life and letters as these raw gems are, the reader walks through the pages and when the gleam of something interesting that "glows with a life of its own" catches the eye, bends over and picks it up. *Oh, yes*, she says, turning it over in her hand and reflecting on it. *I understand what you mean. This reminds me of...* The wisdom in its raw state invites the reader to become a participant in the mining. She is free to enter in imaginatively to discover, polish, find clarity, and ultimately, make it her own.

The journey of Anne Morrow Lindbergh in her diaries and letters is full of these treasures, just waiting to be discovered.

Gifts from the Spirit

Children Aren't Born
to Live Their Parents' Lives

"...I want to go to a different place...to bring back a different view of things to our family...It will take courage to break away from EVERYTHING I have been brought up to love...to go...against everybody's expectations. Oh, I wish to Heaven they'd let me do something STRONG, LET me show that I can stand up alone."

— Letter to sister Elisabeth, BRING ME A UNICORN, pp. 6,7

Poised on the brink of college, Anne's independence asserted itself. She wanted to break away from the Morrow women's tradition of attending Smith College. Her older, more socially confident—and attractive, thought Anne—sister Elisabeth had followed dutifully in her mother's footsteps. Anne was well aware that she was different from her extroverted mother and sister.

Not wishing to be compared with either of them and eager to find her own way, she felt that Vassar, where many of her friends were going, would be a better place for her. She looked to her sister to understand and bolster her courage to take a stand for herself.

But, unfortunately, looking to Elisabeth was looking to the wrong person. Her older sister advised that to go anywhere but Smith would "hurt" their mother. Not surprisingly, Anne acquiesced. Swimming against the tide of family expectation seemed impossible. The passivity behind her plea for permission to be strong and independent was the byproduct of eighteen years of denial of her own personal power. Despite this lack of encouragement, she longed to be her own person—to come out from under the heavy family mantle and stand on her own.

Anne went on to have a successful experience at Smith, earning awards and later honorary degrees there. All the while she buried her anger and resentment. But not so successfully.

Years later, her daughter, Reeve, was unaware of her mother's true feelings about attending Smith. In her moving memoir about growing up as a child of Charles and Anne in *Under a Wing*, Reeve described a surprising conversation when her mother was eighty-three. Reeve was taken aback to realize that, after all the years that had passed, her mother "bitterly...minded her own capitulation."[6]

Anne's struggle with choosing a college and the fall-out from her compliance that lingered throughout her life reminds me as parent that I must be careful to discriminate between my needs and those of my child.

Having Anne follow in her footsteps to Smith must have been enormously gratifying to Anne's mother. But insisting on doing it her way meant her daughter missed an opportunity to spread her wings and find herself as an individual. The task to separate would remain before her—but as always when these developmental tasks are postponed—it would be harder. No wonder Anne was angry.

As well-intentioned parents who want the best for our children we often blindly assume "the best" is synonymous with our own wishes. Too often, unfortunately, our own wishes go unexamined and may have more to do with unrecognized needs we have for reassurance from our children. When our children live out the path we took, or perhaps the path we didn't take but wish we would have, they're living secondary lives at enormous cost to their own well-being.

Each of us is entitled to his or her own life. Period. Children aren't born to live their parents' lives nor to fulfill their parents' conscious or unconscious agenda.

Finding Nourishment
for the Soul in Nature

"Yesterday I sat in a field of violets for a
long long time perfectly still, until I really sank
into it—into the rhythm of the place, I mean
—then when I got up to go home I couldn't
walk quickly or evenly because I was still in
time with that field."

⟿ BRING ME A UNICORN, p. 27

Anne's contemplative nature was evident even as a
young woman. In this letter to her mother from
Smith College she shared her unique response to the
arrival of spring—sitting quietly in a field.

Anne was remarkably attentive. One can imagine
her delight in discovering this field. She was visiting
with friends at the Sophia Smith Homestead. They
walked out into the cool New England spring evening
where the cherry blossoms were bursting all around
them—and the apple blossoms were just about to—and

she suddenly spied the field of white violets. Anne sat down, sinking into the beauty of the ephemeral blossoms. She began to breathe in cadence with the soft evening breeze that gently tossed the violets back and forth. She was transfixed by the delicacy of the fragile white petals against the deep green leaves and grass. Such beauty. Aware that the blossoms were present for a time only and that she had had the good fortune to come upon them filled her with a sense of the preciousness and graciousness of life. This was now. Fully immersed in the moment Anne beheld the exquisiteness of life. It was an eternal moment.

I think I know something of what Anne may have experienced in that field. I'm reminded of when I too was a student in the east.

Princeton, New Jersey was a town right out of a storybook. Full of history and tradition, charm and good taste—not to mention excruciatingly careful zoning laws—Princeton was a place that reminded you, at every turn, of how privileged you were to be there. Its ethos enveloped you the moment you entered the borough. You'd drive past immaculately restored pre-Revolutionary homes, battlefields and monuments to the Revolutionary War, the nobly gothic buildings of the university. You'd pass through tunnels of giant ancient trees that once stood guard over Washington's troops as they marched to Trenton—and you realized that you had arrived at a place that had a distinct and well-cultivated sense of itself. It was here long before you, and would be here long after you left. And *you* would be the only one to change in the meantime.

As uncompromising as it was, though, Princeton had its gifts. Every season there was something to experience. But spring was the one that—if I close my eyes—I can go back and still feel and smell and see.

As a graduate student at Princeton Seminary, I had a room in a dormitory that looked out over Springdale Golf Course. One April evening after dinner I returned to my room to study. The lightness of the evening air hung in sharp contrast to the heavy task before me: three major papers to write and a final exam to prepare for, all due within a week. I sat down at my desk, pushed right up underneath the window that looked out through a mass of pink and white cherry blossoms to the golf course. Probably a big mistake if I really wanted to get some work done. The voices of William James, Søren Kierkegaard, Erik Erikson, Carol Gilligan, and the rest stacked in piles before me clamored for my attention, but I really didn't hear them. I couldn't take my eyes off the scene outside my window.

Inevitably I gave up my attempts to work as I found myself drawn to walk into the evening. The air had a seductive quality that beckoned my senses, telling me that this was something not to be missed. I strolled down the hill behind my dorm and across the narrow College Road that separated the campus from Springdale. The beauty that awaited me was unforgettable.

The gently rolling green hills of the golf course were dotted with flowering trees that practically groaned under the weight of their luxurious pink and white blossoms. The emerald fairways were empty of golfers, and I walked all over, wherever I wanted. In certain spots the trees created canopies of blossoms that hung so low I felt I was in a room of flowers. The gothic and majestic tower of Princeton University's graduate school rising up in the background like Rapunzel's chamber only added to my feeling of being transported to a magical fairy-tale-like land. But it was real.

I was filled with wonder, immersed in the beauty and the sense that we—the blossoms and I—would only be there for a time. I wouldn't always live in this room with the window that overlooks a springtime fairyland. I would graduate and move on. The blossoms would wither and fade as the days grew warmer and green leaves would take over, making it hard to remember the blossoms were ever here. But they would return.

And while I might not be there to see them, I sealed this moment—like Anne's eternal moment—forever in my memory: a gift of beauty and a gentle reminder to listen whenever the spring breeze calls me out.

Struggling to Embrace Her Own True Feelings

"Do you see, Mother? It's such a relief to realize that you don't have to fit yourself to someone else's pattern. Sue, then, gave me a kind of new confidence in my pattern. You see, don't you?"

— BRING ME A UNICORN, p. 27

Anne wasn't alone that spring evening when she discovered the field of violets. Several girlfriends from Smith were with her. She described two of them as "running around like happy colts," their youthful exuberance unleashed in response to the spring in the air. In the past, she wrote her mother, she would have felt like she should do that too. She had often tried to be like them, running and skipping to match the mood of the group. But this evening she declared that she just wanted to quietly take it in, to sit and absorb the beauty of the dusk. Her friend, Sue, told her that that's just what *she* felt like doing. Sue's honesty strengthened Anne's resolve to embrace her own true feelings. It dawned on her that she didn't *have* to do things the way others do, that her own pattern was valid.

You see, Mother, don't you? Unfortunately, Anne's mother didn't. That Anne still struggled as a young woman with the right to have her own feelings and responses reveals that she wasn't granted that growing up. Anne's self-deprecation is woven throughout all the volumes of her diaries and letters. She carried the pattern into her marriage as well. Anne continually struggled to be what her mother and her husband needed her to be for them.

Seeing our children as individuals separate from ourselves is one of the hardest challenges of being a parent. If we were lucky enough to have parents who were able to see us as individuals in our own right—separate and distinct from them—we are more likely to be able to do the same for our children. For those of us who weren't so lucky, the task is much harder. It requires that we do the work that should have happened much earlier—the work of becoming our true self. Not the person someone else wants or needs you to be. The person you really are.

First we must give *ourselves* permission to be ourselves. Then and only then, can we give it to our children.

The Poet, the Pilot, and Their Passion

"The feeling of exultant joy that there is anyone like that in the world...Clouds and stars and birds—I must have been walking with my head down looking at puddles for twenty years."

⌐ BRING ME A UNICORN, p. 99

Anne was a twenty-one year old senior at Smith when she had an encounter that would change her life. It was December of 1927 and the Morrow family was spending the Christmas holidays together in Mexico City, where Anne's father served as U.S. ambassador. It had been just seven months since Charles Lindbergh made his historic solo flight that rocked the world. Now, at the invitation of Ambassador Morrow, and in the interest of strengthening relations between the United States and Mexico, Lindbergh was coming to spend the holidays with the Morrow family. And he was about to rock Anne's world too.

Until this point, Anne's world had included only the New England upper class—the well-to-do, highly educated, and intellectual—her parents' people. Charles was different and he took her breath away. This shy "clear, direct, straight boy"[7] who said little but accomplished much, stood in sharp contrast to all the other men she'd known. Next to Charles—an independent, courageous, sincere, forthright man of action—all the articulate, well-read, sophisticated, pretentious suitors Anne had known paled. His directness, his economy of words, his lack of pretense, and his sheer masculine presence bowled Anne over.

In her world people read about and discussed things. In Charles Lindbergh's world, people *did* them.

The attraction between Anne and Charles was instantaneous and mutual, but it would be several months before Charles called for a date. In the fall of 1928, he invited Anne to fly with him. Within a few months they were engaged, and in May of 1929 they married.

Despite their whirlwind courtship, Anne was racked with doubts, and she agonized over their relationship: "It is a dream and a mistake. We are utterly opposed."[8] She was introspective; he was a man of action. She was an incessant reader; he rarely cracked a book, his idea of good poetry was that of the low-brow, sentimental Robert Service, and he didn't even *get* the cartoons in *The New Yorker* magazine. She was Ivy League; he was a college dropout. She was a dreamer; he was practical.

Yet underneath it all there was a powerful attraction. As their daughter Reeve said years later, their marriage was inevitable.[9]

Indeed it was. For what was at the heart of the attraction between Anne and Charles was a deep, unconscious connection: their emotional similarity.

Years later Anne described a conversation she and Charles had with the Duke and Duchess of Windsor at a party in Paris before the war. The four compared notes on the isolation and indignation they suffered because of their fame: "—a pair of unicorns meeting another pair of unicorns."[10]

Anne's self-identified image of the unicorn—an elusive magical creature—was one that would recur in her literary work. The volume of diaries and letters that contained her first meeting of Charles was entitled *Bring Me a Unicorn*. Her only published volume of poetry, *The Unicorn*, included a long poem called "The Unicorn in Captivity," which was inspired by a tapestry from the Metropolitan Museum of Art. In the poem Anne described a hunted, fenced in, bound, and wounded creature who found his freedom internally—an image that resonated deeply with her.

The themes of captivity and freedom surfaced again and again in the Lindberghs' lives. This appeared to be because of the relentless pressure of fame. Incessant publicity held them captive, rendering them unable to move freely. Flying and escaping to far corners of the world granted them the freedom they craved.

I believe that for Anne and Charles, though, the pull toward freedom and away from captivity stemmed from origins far deeper than the world of fame they inhabited as adults. Their identification with the wounded creature was rooted in the pain and "captivity" of emotional isolation they each experienced as children.

Charles's parents were estranged during his childhood, but they never divorced. At a young age he was forced to assume adult responsibilities and was expected to grow up quickly. One senses that there was no one really there to take care of *him*. Living in a chronically painful situation, Charles learned early not to feel things. Action became his means of escape.

Anne had a family that appeared to offer every possible good thing to its children, but her childhood, too, was marked by emotional deprivation. She was expected to grow up to be just like her mother—a woman who was uncomfortable with her own feelings and who avoided them through nonstop social activity and philanthropy. Anne was not supported in becoming *herself*.

When Anne and Charles met that December in Mexico, each of them unconsciously recognized themselves in each other. A unicorn meeting another unicorn. A powerful attraction.

In her novel, *The Names of the Mountains,* Reeve Lindbergh told a fictionalized version of her aging mother's gradual decline. Anne—through the character Alicia in the story—said marriage was "...both an escape from and a reflection of the marriage in which each partner was raised."[11]

For Anne, marriage to Charles was certainly both. He offered an escape from the intellectualized, protective, and confined world of her parents. Charles offered adventure and a chance for her to shift from the life of the mind to the life of the body. Anne's decision to marry Charles stretched her in ways she might never have known had she not taken the leap.

What she didn't realize, though, was that she was marrying into the same emotional reality that she had grown up with. Life with Charles may have looked different externally, but emotionally, she would discover, he was every bit as detached as her own parents.

The mystery of attraction is really not so mysterious after all. More and more, I believe that we are attracted to people—romantically or otherwise—at this deeply unconscious level. There is something about the person we are attracted to, below the flow of words and actions, that—no matter how different from us they may appear—is familiar. That reminds us of what we already know.

Not only do we find relationships that replicate the emotional reality we knew growing up, we also manage to create circumstances that repeat it, too. Anne married a man who mirrored the emotional distance and exacting demands of her parents. She also found herself in circumstances, due to her celebrity, in which she had to struggle against feelings of isolation, misperceptions, and captivity—evoking a sense of reality not unlike that of a little girl whose identity and value is not perceived accurately by those around her.

As adults we recreate the hurts of childhood to get a second chance to work them out and be free of them. And we do all this without realizing it, of course. What is deepest and truest in us is wiser than our conscious self and longs for us to be healed.

But healing doesn't come automatically, nor does it come easily.

We gain our second chance only when we have the courage to allow this deeper knowledge to come into the light. This requires the slow, painful work of choosing to understand ourselves and the reality of our history. Only then can the present circumstances—the marriage, the difficult situation—be apprehended in its proper perspective and be transformed.

The Key to Making Her Life Count

"It seems to me...that if you really and sincerely and passionately want to do something (and wholeheartedly, with your sincerest self) it is by doing that that you will be most useful, will be giving the most, will be of individual value."

⌐ BRING ME A UNICORN, p. 124

Anne wrestled interminably with the pressure of living up to the Morrow family code of service to others. An introvert in a household of high-achieving extroverts, she felt bound to find a way to live up to her family's expectations. As a college student and not long after her first encounter with Charles Lindbergh, she was struck with this new thought: that following her desires was the key to making her life count.

Lindbergh was the perfect example. When he undertook the planning and execution of his New York-to-

Paris flight he did so because he *wanted* to. An inner fire fueled his drive, not some extrinsic ideal of advancing the fledgling world of aviation or going down in history as an aviation pioneer; these were by-products of his accomplishment. But they would not have happened had he lacked the passion for this feat. There was something deeply personal about his need to fly the Atlantic solo. His daughter Reeve jokes today that she thinks the truth is he did it "to get away from his mother."[12]

I wonder how many accomplished people are driven by motivations less pretty and more complicated than they'd care to admit. I'll bet most are. Of course, we like to see ourselves in the best possible light, so we reach for lofty, altruistic rationales for our choices. Politics is not the only realm for spin; it's inherent to being human.

Until my son was three years old I stayed home with him as a full-time mom. Those were precious, fleeting years that I look back on and treasure. In those days, when questioned about when I would be returning to work, I bristled and defended my choice as the right thing for my son and for me. Isn't he better off with a mom who is home and there for him rather than at some impersonal day-care center or with a babysitter who doesn't have the same feeling for him that I do? I knew his early years would go quickly and I wanted to be there.

These were things I believed—and still do. But underneath my conscious awareness, at a deeper level that had nothing to do with my son or my desire to be a good mother, the truth was part of me was afraid to get back out there and carve out a life that was separate and mine. My choice to stay home was a complicated mix of good intentions and unrecognized fears.

Anne's words remind me that embracing the desires of my heart is the key to fulfillment and finding my place with others. Being directed by outer forces—the expectations of others, the desire to be or do good, fitting into a role, a worthy cause, making money, etc.—may carry me along for a time. But the end result is dissatisfaction, energy depletion, depression, alienation from myself and, inevitably, from others. It is, in short, spiritual death.

Looking inward means discovering the truth about myself. When I am free to go where my passions lead me I find myself on the road to self-fulfillment, impacting not only myself, but my relationships, and my place in the world. I think this is what it means to follow a "calling." It is to be true to who we are in our deepest selves.

The Hope of Spring
in Her Spirit

"Forsythia is pure joy. There is not an ounce, not a glimmer of sadness or even knowledge in forsythia. Pure, undiluted, untouched joy."
— BRING ME A UNICORN, p. 138

It's been too many years since I've lived in a climate that supported forsythia. We don't have them in Southern California. But I remember them in New Jersey, where they lined the highways in a blast of yellow in the spring, and I remember them before that, in Missouri where I grew up.

We had a forsythia bush in my backyard, down by the creek that flowed at the bottom of the property. As a child I didn't try to learn the names of trees or bushes, but I absorbed many of them from hearing my parents talk. My mother always remarked about the forsythia when its yellow buds began to swell. "Oh, the forsythia's almost out." Or "Oh, the forsythia is out." She would comment on the progress of the forsythia as she looked out the kitchen window while doing the dishes. I knew these simple statements meant something. She was on the lookout for spring. For some reason my parents never planted daffodils, so forsythia was the harbinger of spring at our house.

My mother must have loved forsythia. It meant that the long tedium of winter was over. She was a housewife with a husband and three children and a house to take care of, and one of her supreme joys was escaping it all to go shopping, or play bridge, or go to her garden club. Long cold winters and snow cramped her freedom. Spring also meant she could go back to hanging wash outside instead of in the basement, as she did when it was cold. She didn't believe in using her dryer much.

I miss the miracle of spring. Living in a climate where flowers and trees bloom all year long is a lovely thing. But I miss the drama of the cycle of death and rebirth borne out in four seasons. Spring pushing up out of the bleak, harsh, dead of winter is hope epitomized. When you live in it, you feel indwelt by it somehow. After the long tedium of dull, cold winter you feel lighter, buoyed in optimism, warmed and reassured of renewal deep in the marrow of your bones.

One Easter Anne reflected that the signs of spring are the Resurrection made visible: a reminder that no matter what, there is love and beauty and goodness and spirit in the world.

Not an ounce...of sadness or even knowledge in forsythia... Yellow clouds of forsythia blossoms rest lightly on their slender branches, bursting in color against the grass beginning to green again, unaware of its own importance—what it means to a world dormant in gray.

The Heart Behind the Facade

"A little appreciation seems to me even more insidious than a little learning. It taints everything it touches and it touches everything, just the veneer of appreciation."

— BRING ME A UNICORN, p. 147

Anne had just returned from an unsatisfactory date with a boy from Amherst, whom she described as "a mass of conventions—his talk, his ideas, his clothes, his car." He was nice and good-natured enough, but his attempts to appear cultured and create an impression rang false and spoiled the possibility of Anne's interest. This mediocre date came just months after Anne's first meeting with Charles, the "clear, direct, straight boy" who made no attempts at pretense. "How it has swept out of sight all other men I have known, all the pseudo-intellectuals, the sophisticates, the posers—all the arty people."[13]

Anne was taken with Charles—partly because with him she sensed that what you see is what you get. With Charles there was no dross; he was comfortable in his own skin, had no need to appear to be other than who he was. She felt she had met a man of unusual integrity. He didn't have a college degree, didn't read books, didn't speak the language of the world of Smith College, but it didn't matter. He was a man who knew who he was; even the adulation that surrounded him after his flight hadn't turned his head.

I understand that longing for something to be all of a piece, as Anne would say, whether it's with people or things. I want things to be the same on the inside, as they appear to be on the outside. There's always the pang of disappointment when it turns out not to be so.

I've run across people with "the veneer of appreciation" too often in religious, psychological, and academic circles: people who have and use language about truth, but are in reality far from knowing it themselves.

A friend of mine had a religion and philosophy professor at her small liberal arts college whose main passion—the theological theme—woven through all his classes, was the love of God. But he far from embodied that. This professor ran the classroom like a prison camp. If you came to class late he'd stop his lecture and glare at you darkly. That's if you were lucky. If you weren't so lucky he'd throw a barb your way along with the glare. He frequently belittled students' questions during class and insulted them. My friend remembers sitting in his class trying not to call attention to herself. She was so terrified of ending up on the other end of his wrath that once when she was running late she simply didn't go to class at all, rather than risk his hostility. She hated to miss that lecture, though, because the subject matter was so compelling. We used to laugh together about the irony of it.

I don't any more. As I get older, I have less patience with this lack of self awareness, because it's so damaging. People with all the right words but none of the emotional reality behind them can be powerfully seductive. They pull you toward them with the promise that they are who they seem to be, that they understand what's important. But when you get closer, you see that the words are a facade, a cover for their own emptiness. There is nothing there.

I am learning to avoid those who speak too easily about what is important. Glibness is a sign to me that the speaker is often far away from knowing the thing deeply. The chasm between knowledge of the head and knowledge of the heart does, as Anne says, taint everything it touches.

Life is Found in the Shadow of Death

"It does seem so discouragingly sad to me: rooms get dusty and clothes always need mending and flowers fade and teeth decay. It's always like that."

— BRING ME A UNICORN, p. 159

Anne was a Smith College co-ed living away from home in the dorm when she was struck by it. It's all around us, really, if only we have eyes to see it. The material world is in a state of slowly breaking down right before our eyes. Everywhere are reminders that we—and most of the things in our world—are taking up space only temporarily here. Appliances break down, paint peels, upholstery fades, weeds encroach, clothes become dated and worn, hair grays, wrinkles appear and flesh sags, cars lose their luster and new-car smell, cuticles get ragged, carpets wear out, children grow up too fast. Nothing stays the same.

And we rail against this. Unconsciously, of course. But we rail all the same. We work so hard to tend all of these things. To slow down the process of deterioration that is all around us, to shield ourselves from these omnipresent signs of change and decline. My parents called this "upkeep"; things just require a lot of upkeep.

The unbearable is latent everywhere, even in beauty. Anne wrote: "The lilacs are faded. I detest dead flowers and throwing them away and the putrid, scummy water. It is almost better not to have them. I hate—it really hurts—to see them fade. I pretend they're not faded and give them cold baths and look the other way when I see them drooping. It's no good—they *always* fade!"[14]

Dusty rooms, frayed clothes, dead flowers. Perhaps what's so unsettling about them is they remind us that we, too, are in the process of deterioration. Hideous thought. The idea of our own non-existence is anathema to us. Nearly impossible to contemplate, we can light on it for a nanosecond, perhaps, but we can't linger. It's unthinkable—that someday we won't be here.

So we do all kinds of things to stave off the reminders, to push away the signs that life is short and unbearably precious.

I saw a "Twilight Zone" episode once in which a character made the choice to be eternally young. He would marry a woman, and as she grew old and frail and he didn't, he would leave her and move on to a younger model. Pathetically, his choice meant he lost his ability to truly love and appreciate a woman. He was chastised by a wiser man who reminded him that we appreciate a rose *because* we know it will only bloom and be beautiful for a time. Its very transitoriness is what evokes the depth of feeling we have for it.

As much as we are repelled by death and do a pretty good job of denying it in its many forms, large and small, its shadow is what gives life its poignancy. The truth is the more we let in the awareness that our stay here is brief, the more richly we live. In her novel *The Steep Ascent*, Anne wrote of those who are able to live with the awareness of the shadow: "We see death behind each blade of grass, like a shadow accenting it. So incredibly beautiful, so sharp, so clear does this shadow make the blade of grass that one cries out for joy."[15]

I can't live in this awareness all the time, but when I let it in, when I contemplate that the moment I'm now in—whatever it's filled with—will be gone, never to return I find I do live more appreciatively. Standing at the kitchen sink doing the dishes yet again, hearing the *Rugrats* theme song blaring from the TV for the umpteenth time as my son plays with his Legos strewn all over the living room, I remind myself that what feels mundane and interminable now I will look back on as infinitely precious simply because it is no more. Before I know it my son will be more interested in meeting girls and going out with his friends and the living room floor that I couldn't find a place to walk on because it was covered in Legos will be bare and empty.

But we are heartbreakingly fragile in our ability to be aware. Anne was struck by this as she watched Thornton Wilder's play, *Our Town*.[16] The main character, Emily, is dead, yet she is granted one day in which she can return to the living. Finding herself back in the midst of an ordinary day of her childhood, she cries out to those she loves who are so caught up in going about their business that they are oblivious to appreciating what is right in front of them: "It goes so fast. We don't have time to look at each other...Do any human beings ever realize life while they live it?"[17]

No, we can't always be conscious of our treasure. But we can—as Anne ultimately learned to in the wake of tragedy—savor the moments and cultivate our awareness, that our lives as we know them are finite. Not an easy thought to hold, but one that just may enable us to realize the gift before us.

The Way Life Should Be

"I am writing you in the desperate feeling that we will never get to North Haven. I have felt superstitious about it from the beginning because I have counted on it overmuch all summer long: the quiet and apartness and all of you, and the feeling of being completely alone and natural and oneself..."

⟶ HOUR OF GOLD, HOUR OF LEAD, p. 72

Anne was a newly married bride of twenty-four when she wrote these words to her mother. After the wedding and honeymoon in May she and Charles had barely touched back down to earth. His involvement in the aviation industry beckoned him from all quarters of the country. It was an exciting time for Anne, joining him in these ventures. She was meeting new people, seeing parts of the country she'd never seen before, and adjusting to life with her new husband. But she missed her family and longed for something familiar and secure in the midst of her new transient life.

Since she was a young girl, Anne had vacationed with her family in the summer on the island of North Haven, just off the coast of Maine. Their large summer "cottage" overlooked Penobscot Bay with a view to the blue Camden Hills on the mainland. For Anne, North Haven offered a retreat, a chance to be with her family away from the usual rhythms of life. Whether North Haven delivered long, lazy summer days in the cool clear sunshine or cozy indoor hours by the fire as squalls swirled outside, the Morrow summer home was a refuge. Here, Anne's parents were relieved from some of the pressures of their busy lives and the family was free to simply be.

This first summer of her marriage Anne feared she might not get there. For the first time she experienced the tug of the needs of her husband on one hand and the pull of her family on the other. It was a tension she would feel always. Becoming caught in what others close to her wanted from her, to the extent that she had difficulty claiming what she wanted for herself, was a familiar place.

In the midst of this dynamic, however, I'm sure that Anne herself longed to get back to North Haven that summer.

If you've ever been to North Haven you'd understand why.

When I lived on the East Coast I had a friend whose family owned two summer cottages on North Haven. My friend, Laurel, had grown up spending summers on the island, just as Anne had. One summer she invited me and a few other friends to go to North Haven for a long weekend. I was just discovering Anne Morrow Lindbergh's books, so I already knew of the island and was thrilled for the opportunity to go.

It turned out to be beyond my ability to imagine. A sign posted along the highway just past the state line says: "Welcome to Maine: The Way Life Should Be." That captures perfectly the way I have come to feel about North Haven. Over the next several summers, the island would be a yearly vacation retreat for me and a group of friends from Princeton.

Regardless of the weather, North Haven was magical. Otherworldly. Whether cloudy and rainy and shrouded in mists of purple, blue, and gray, or bathed in sunshine and cool crystalline air, the deep green pines stood out against the wild rocky shore and beckoned you to come closer, go deeper. The scent of pine and sea filled your lungs and you felt more alive than ever.

Our trip was the same from year to year. The ferry delivered us into the arms of the harbor and gently let us go. We drove through fields of blue lupine and grazing cows to get to our cottage. The lilacs by the porch would still be in bloom. I'd cut some for the table that night. We'd unpack, stopping every couple of minutes to look out the bedroom window into the cove just yards from the front door. Across the cove, the sun would just be beginning to dip behind the Camden Hills in a spectacular display of reds, oranges, pinks, and magentas. We'd all stop what we were doing to rush out to the pier to watch. This became one of our rituals on the island.

We had others, and a sort of routine emerged. Since there were so few distractions on the island we'd make up our own. First were the lazy mornings. People would rise whenever they felt like it. Someone would make coffee, and there were usually a few people sitting on the porch drinking it, reading novels, and having leisurely conversations. Someone might cook a big breakfast, or we might fend for ourselves when hunger struck. Grape-Nuts and muffins were perfect. Once children came along, breakfasts became a bit more official. After breakfast, someone might take a walk or a bike ride. Or go sailing. Or row across the cove to the spit of rocks to dig mussels for dinner. Or sunbathe. The water in the cove was too cold to swim in, but Laurel took one quick dip every year. She'd been doing it since she was a little girl.

Lunch was a loose affair, too. A pot of homemade soup sat on the stove, ready whenever we were. Afterward there might be naps outside in the sun. Someone might make a trip to town to restock supplies at Waterman's, the only general store on the island, or to pick up lobster, fresh from this morning's haul, for dinner that night. We'd scatter alone or in couples or small groups to do whatever we felt like. But late afternoon brought a ritual nobody wanted to miss.

As the sun dipped lower and the air grew cooler, we pulled on our sweaters and took up our mallets. The lawn in front of the cottage that sloped to the edge of the cove became our croquet court. It was happy hour. Steve would roll out the old battered wooden wagon of some child long ago and set up the bar. Gin and tonics. Margaritas. Take your pick. Music rolled out over the lawn—James Taylor, maybe, or the soundtrack to "The Big Chill." As a matter of fact, sometimes we felt we were living "The Big Chill." We'd sip our drinks; we'd savor the sunset; we'd dance and sing along to the music; we'd have no mercy for each other on the court, sending each other's croquet balls off into oblivion and evoking the *ooga-booga* charm of protection around our own (this involved making the sign of the cross over your croquet ball and chanting *ooga booga*) whenever threatened. We were silly and laughed at nothing and everything. Whoever was responsible for dinner that night would be inside preparing the lobster and it would be ready soon. Life was good.

Our days took on a lovely timeless rhythm. Our spirits adapted to our surroundings and we breathed in time with the wind and the tides and our most basic needs. Released from the pressures of our day-to-day existence, we felt more fully alive than ever. Our sense of life was heightened—perhaps because we had slowed down enough to appreciate it.

The special group of friends are scattered all across the country now. We had been in graduate school together, some of us worked at a summer camp together, some of us had been to college together. One of us has died, children have been born. We've all moved to new stages in our lives. But none of us will forget those days. Even in the midst of living them I think we all knew how extraordinary our days on North Haven were. We were young, on the threshold of the rest of our lives, and our playground was one of the loveliest places God ever made.

Mystical, enchanting, ruggedly beautiful, North Haven is a taste of what heaven might just be like. Or at the very least—the way life was intended to be. I can understand Anne's worry that she might not get back there. But she did. And as she would recount later in *Gift From the Sea*, she managed to find "North Haven" for herself in other places. too. Places where she could retreat to and, in letting go of the demands of daily life, tap into her inner springs once again.

What is This Thing That is Presence and Yet Not Presence?

"My boy is so far away, even here [at her mother's home]—until I went upstairs. As I walked into his room...everything came back. I looked at his toys, the rooster, the Swedish horse...the little blue stool, his cart of blocks ...Then the bureau drawers—each one so full of him. Just the familiarity of my hand on the crib seemed to put him back there. What is this thing that is presence and yet not presence? I went down crying but more satisfied.

⌐ HOUR OF GOLD, HOUR OF LEAD, pp. 257-258

Anne made this diary entry just eleven days after she learned that her infant son had been killed. Charles A. Lindbergh Jr. was stolen from his crib at the Lindbergh's Hopewell, New Jersey, farmhouse in March of 1932. After two months of raised and dashed hopes for his safe return, the eighteen-month-old child's body was discovered half-buried in a wooded area less than five miles from their home. He never lived beyond the night he was taken.

Six months pregnant with her second child, Anne was visiting her mother's home, where she and her husband and child had lived while they waited for their own home to be built. They had not been back since baby Charlie's death. Anne tiptoed upstairs and gently opened the door to her son's room. She was flooded with more than memories: she felt his presence. The smell of the tin of Johnson's baby powder, the little crushed blue jacket he wore over his sleeping suit when he came downstairs to play every night, his gray pussycat with the tail nearly off. In each of these things, she found her baby. She stole back downstairs in silent tears, but was comforted. He didn't feel so far away.

"What is this thing that is presence and yet not presence?" Visiting my mother in St. Louis a few months after my father's death, this question became real for me. I was there for our annual summertime sojourn, the first time I'd been home since his funeral the winter before. I lived in California now, and the geographical distance had buffered the realization that he was gone. Intellectually I knew he was, of course. But, emotionally, it wasn't entirely real; when you don't see someone regularly you don't meet the person's absence as sharply as you do when you live nearby.

While I knew there would be a reckoning with this trip, it didn't come right away or in any way I expected.

I didn't apprehend the reality of his death in the places I thought I would. Not in his empty, dark blue, leather recliner, situated in the best possible location in the family room for TV viewing. This was the "dad" chair, reserved for him with unspoken understanding all the years I was growing up and into the present—except when his grandson came to visit. My son was granted a special dispensation to park there for his morning cartoons.

I didn't find it either when I sat at the desk in his study. He'd sit there to read the paper while his grandson took over his armchair in the family room. Tipping back in his swivel chair, with drugstore reading glasses perched on the edge of his handsome nose, my father would peruse the *St. Louis Post-Dispatch*—even if it was the liberal paper that knocked the *Globe-Democrat* out of business.

I didn't realize the fact of his death, either, in what would have been his empty place at the table. Just as his chair had the best view in the room for seeing the television, my father had the best view in the breakfast nook, the place he and my mother took their meals. At his place you could look out a bay window onto a pastoral scene where horses grazed in a field that touched their property. Now my mother moved my older brother, who was also visiting, into this spot. (If it sounds like the men in my family get preferential treatment, it's because they do.) So even his absence at the dinner table didn't strike me deeply.

That my father was permanently gone did not become real to me until several days into the visit, when I ventured downstairs into the basement. That's where it hit me.

I slipped quietly down the carpeted basement stairs. (Yes, carpeted. My father was the kind of man who not only carpeted his basement stairs, but also regularly vacuumed the concrete basement floor.) Instinctively, I made my way over to his workbench.

My dad built his workbench when he and my mother bought their first house. They had moved twice since, and never left the workbench behind.

Standing in front of it now, I pictured it in the tiny laundry room it occupied when I was four, and then later in the larger laundry room in the house where I grew up. It was a permanent fixture in the life of our family. It was the place where things that needed to be repaired were piled, where shoes that needed shining were shined, where my father could often be seen hunched over, working his magic on some electrical gizmo (his favorite word of choice) that needed overhauling.

I grew up believing that my father could fix anything.

Years later, when my parents moved to the new house, he would take my son downstairs to the basement and let him tinker with him at his workbench. I can still see my preschool-age son perched atop a sturdy plastic drum of laundry detergent before scraps of discarded wood, drilling holes with the old manual drill that had belonged to his great-grandfather, and hammering nails with his grandfather's tack hammer—right alongside his Granddad. Some summers they would make special projects together. One year it was a birdhouse; another, it was a cement-and-tile steppingstone for the garden.

Although I stood alone at that moment with my memories rushing at me, I was surrounded by my father's presence. He was there.

There, in the stained, scuffed surface of his workbench where he had polished shoes, built Pinewood Derby cars, repaired lamps, painted furniture, framed pictures, fixed the cord on my mother's iron, and completed innumerable other tasks which kept the surface of our lives functioning smoothly. And each tool, hanging in its spot on the pegboard of his workbench just where he'd left it, was full of him.

I was overwhelmed by his presence. And I knew, for the first time, that he was gone. The reality that I hadn't been able to access before came now. And along with the tears that came from deep inside my body came the knowledge of what he had meant to me.

My father was a man who wasn't comfortable with his feelings and didn't share them easily, and so he showed that he cared in practical ways. Building, repairing, improving, fixing—he loved to do all of these things and we received the benefits. Here was a man who showed care through his handiness. He was able to love through doing the thing *he* loved. My loss became real that summer day because in my father's workbench I found his essence.

"What is this thing that is presence and yet not presence?" Anne asked. It may be this: We inhabit the things we love and, even in death, if we have loved we leave some of ourselves behind.

Embracing Grief
as a Path to Peace

"I feel as though I wanted just to sit in the sun, outdoors, and let waves of green oak leaves and waves of small insect sounds, small rustlings and stirrings, pour into me, fill up all the wrinkles and cracks, make a smooth blank surface over everything. Then let impressions and thoughts come back clearly on that satin surface. But I do not want now to read or think or work; I just want to be filled up to the brim with quiet."

— HOUR OF GOLD, HOUR OF LEAD, p. 261

Just eighteen days before she wrote this, the body of Anne's baby was discovered in the woods near her home. She sat in the protected garden of her mother's estate, in the early throes of grief. She was carrying her second child, and nurturing thoughts about turning her diaries and letters from the survey flight she and Charles made the year before into a book. It would be called *North to the Orient*, but it would have to wait. She had other more important work to do now. She had grieving to do.

How well I know the need to be still and give myself over to the elements—sun and air and sky—to be washed clean and emptied so that I can be filled up again with the quiet she speaks of, the strength of my own spirit.

A few days ago I returned from a family holiday gathering in Las Vegas where my brother Craig lives. While I love my brother and enjoy seeing him, I consider Las Vegas to be a soul-defying experience. The ersatz quality of the place is just not my thing. And gambling to me is a foreign concept—like throwing money on the floor, as my brother's friend Johanna used to say. Just getting there—spending seven and a half hours in traffic that should be a four-and-a-half hour drive—is trial enough. But the holiday was overshadowed this year by more than just these wrinkles.

It was the first Christmas without my father, who had passed away earlier in the year. Before that our family had sustained multiple losses within a short space of time. Our brother Gary had died a few years earlier. My other brother Craig had recently ended a twenty-year relationship, and I had gone through a difficult divorce. I felt weighed down with layers of loss and despair. Our family had changed so drastically in such a short time. The ghosts of Christmases past were all around us—yet not really acknowledged.

If there is anything worse than loss, it is not being able to share it with those closest to you. When you're in a family that isn't comfortable with difficult feelings, those feelings stay trapped under your skin until you're so constricted you can't move or breathe freely. I'm convinced it's not loss itself that cripples people, it's the refusal to grieve it.

I returned from my trip to a week of solitude. My son went to his dad's for their holiday time together, and I planned to write. Not surprisingly, I wasn't able to return to it until I gave myself time to take things in. I had bottled up the feelings of a week and needed an outlet.

I might have written Anne's passage myself. I sat on the patio in my backyard, surrounded by pine trees, pots of purple and yellow pansies and blue and white lobelia, soaking up the warmth of the Southern California December sun. I put my reclining lawn chair back and my feet up. I didn't want to do anything. I didn't want to go anywhere. I just wanted to *be*. I might put some music on. Or I might not. Sometimes music demands too much, and I wanted nothing commanding my attention. I did this until I didn't need to do it anymore. The feelings moved through me, and I let myself have them. And slowly, slowly—I began to feel my self that had felt so far away come back. I felt stronger. And I could go back to life again.

Grief is an occupation that I'm learning not to side-step. I find it to be a positive, proactive response to pain. Contrary to our culture that encourages us to put our feelings aside and just "get over it," embracing grief is facing reality. When I give myself over to it, grief becomes a river carrying me along, not always easily. The undercurrents can pull at me and drag me under, tossing me so that I can't always tell up from down. But ultimately, the journey smoothes out and I am cleaned out and stronger, filled up with more of myself than I had before. I become, like Anne, "filled up to the brim with quiet" and the sense of being gently upheld by something gracious and bigger than I am.

The Exhilaration of Being Yourself

"It becomes increasingly difficult to talk to people with whom I cannot be completely honest. It is exhausting to do it..."

— LOCKED ROOMS AND OPEN DOORS, p. 266

Once the Lindberghs discovered they could never again live in their home in Hopewell after the kidnapping, they made their permanent home base at Next Day Hill, Anne's mother's estate in Englewood, New Jersey. During this time they were away frequently, traveling extensively. But when they were home, Anne found herself, reluctantly, swept up in her mother's lifestyle.

Life at Next Day Hill involved a steady stream of guests. From organizational meetings with large numbers of people coming through the front door, to a small number of family friends turning up at the lunch or dinner table, Anne frequently found herself forced to interact with people when it wasn't her choice to do so.

Of course it *was* her choice to be living with her family in her mother's home. Anne and Charles believed Betty Morrow's home offered protection they couldn't find elsewhere. Terrorized by the events of 1930, they were now receiving threats against their young son Jon. Unconsciously, of course, there were other reasons these grown adults found themselves "going home." But to them it felt that they had no other options.

Anne was without even a private haven to let down and be herself. When she was out in the world she was "Mrs. Charles Lindbergh," and, because of the incessant publicity, she was highly aware of the need to move and speak discreetly. There was no place for her to simply let down her guard.

While Anne's situation was dramatic, the need to have people with whom you can "let your guard down" and be real is common to us all.

The more people like this that I have in my life—people with whom I can be myself—the less I am inclined to tolerate or devote time to those with whom I can't. The contrast in the interaction is so striking. The former is energizing, the latter depleting.

When is it that I can't be myself? When I feel I'm being judged. When I feel criticized. When I feel unseen or unheard. When I feel I'm not respected. When I feel I must fit an image someone else has of me. When I feel I need to prop up or take care of the other person in some way because—without even putting words to it—everything in him or her asks me to do so.

So I smile, I act, I am forced to distance myself from my real feelings and thoughts because everything I say and do must be second-guessed and screened through the view of that person before I can act or speak. The energy that's required to do all of this is considerable. Exhaustion is inevitable.

At one point as a young girl, Anne experienced the freedom of living otherwise. She wrote in her diary, "I am having the most exhilarating time saying and acting just as I feel and think, lately—speaking when and what I want and keeping quiet when I want and saying to myself with a daredevil feeling, 'Oh well, that's me. If they don't like it, so much the better to know now!'"[18] If Anne's upbringing had supported her in living and speaking out of who she truly was, she wouldn't have struggled so with giving herself the freedom to live that way as an adult. When a child is taught that she must meet the expectations of her parents at the expense of herself, she will continue to do this in her adult relationships. It will be hard work to recognize that it's not only okay, it's imperative to be yourself. To live otherwise, is to deny the truth of who we are at our core, which exacts a high price. Our spirits shrink and atrophy, and our life is reduced to going through the motions without passion.

I love her defiant declaration: "Oh well, that's me...If they don't like it, so much the better to know now!" The freedom, the self-acceptance, and self-love implied in that sentence is a reminder to me that my first responsibility is to be true to myself. And then I can let go of living out of the expectations of others.

Moments of
Heightened Awareness

"I was happy...as though I had recovered everything ever lost, as though I had everything—everything worth having. And I tried to know why, to keep something from this moment of ecstasy, some secret to comfort me when I came down to the human world again."

—— HOUR OF GOLD. HOUR OF LEAD, pp. 312-313

Anne was at the controls of the small plane in which Charles taught her to fly. He was in the plane too, but she was doing the flying. They approached North Haven, the first time they would have been there since the summer before. A year ago they'd touched down for a brief visit to say goodbye to her family and to have one last moment with their baby, Charles Jr., who would be looked after by Anne's mother while they were on their extended flight over the North Pole to the Orient.

Since then, Anne had lost both her father and her baby son.

Full of their absence, she drew nearer to the islands, secretly suspecting they too might be gone. So much of what she'd taken for granted, counted on, loved, had been rocked, shaken, taken from her, why not this too? But no, they were all still there. Just as they'd always been. Just as she knew now, they always would be. In fact, she could see things from here in a way she'd never seen them before. The way her point on the island fit into the bay, the way the group of islands which had seemed so separate before were actually one. She had a vantage point from her cockpit she'd never had before.

Then she dipped closer, looked down on the Morrow house and saw her mother and sister Elisabeth, "two tiny figures clinging together on the lawn." Her heart swelled with pity for them in their frailty and humanness. She knew their pain and their vulnerability. It was just like her own. But they had no idea, no idea at all of the view she had from here.

It was a transcendent moment. From the air Anne glimpsed the intersection of the eternal and the human and realized that despite the uncertainty of life with its disappointments and losses, we are upheld by goodness. The islands and the way they fit together reminded her of this knowledge already within her. She saw their interrelatedness in a way she never had before and grasped that *even when it doesn't seem so* there is a divinity that holds our lives—including the lives of her mother and her sister, so small and vulnerable, down below. Her heart was full of love as she looked down on them from her place in the sky, aching that they didn't have the perspective she now had.

When Anne came down to earth again, she felt the wind cold on her face through her tears. She'd been crying. If only she could have this height, this perspective always, she thought. But she was back in the human world again. The near and familiar. Her losses still hurt. She would miss her father; the pain of losing her son would never leave her. Though she didn't know it yet, her sister Elisabeth would die soon too. Yet, this moment had given her a gift. A glimpse, a reminder that all of our lives—no matter how dark or confused—are held by a compassionate benevolence we don't understand.

I've had this kind of moment. More than once. And I've observed it in others.

You're in the pit of despair. What you've loved, counted on, depended on, is gone. The ground under your feet is no longer solid. Instead it is shifting, rocking—maybe no longer even there. What you loved has died—and part of you has died too.

In this state of being alive but feeling dead, your defenses are down. Those things that normally help you hold your world together just don't work the same way anymore. You are at your most vulnerable. And then comes the gift.

It's as though you stand before a window and someone comes along and pulls aside the curtains and says, "Look! Open your eyes and look around you and see how exquisitely beautiful the world is. Life is unbearably short. Nothing lasts forever. There is sadness and there is loss, but *you* are alive—and your life will go quickly. Live it while you can."

You are granted this moment. You see clearly. And then you have a choice. You can pull the curtains closed and start again to build up your defenses against the pain inside you, feeling less and less and dying on the inside. Or—you can choose to keep the curtains open so that you can let in both the richness and sadness of life. And that means feeling more and more. More sadness, but more joy too.

These moments of heightened awareness come to all of us. If we have the courage, we can, like Anne, bring them back to the "human world" again and allow them to infuse us with the strength to choose life, even in the midst of pain and loss.

Looking For Her True Home

"When a married daughter goes back to live at home, a curious unconscious regression seems to occur. Despite the best intentions on both sides, the old patterns for mother and daughter tend to take over."

— LOCKED ROOMS AND OPEN DOORS, p. xxi

Personally, I don't think regression requires moving back in. Just a visit will do. Ask any of your friends, married or single, who "go home" for Christmas vacation. Grown up children everywhere know about the three-day limit. Hang around longer than three days at your own risk. Anyone can be on her best behavior for three days. Stay longer than that and you're pushing your luck. It's like that wise saying: "Houseguests are like fish. Keep them around longer than three days and they start to smell."

There may actually be a shorter waiting period for families. The old patterns—particularly the unhealthy ones that go unrecognized—are latent, hiding just below the surface, ready to spring forth at the slightest provocation. A look, a gesture, a word. That's all it takes. And there you are. Forty-something with a child, a career, a mortgage, and maybe even the respect of your community—but inside you're fifteen again. And worse, you're acting like it.

I have a mother who *did* for us. A full-time housewife, she took her responsibilities to care for her family's physical needs very seriously. And she did it well. My mother cooked huge meals and we always had multiple dessert choices, all homemade too. "Let's see, do you want the chocolate layer cake, the pineapple upside-down cake or fruit and chocolate chip cookies tonight?"

(*Sigh*) "...Mom, I was really hoping for carrot cake."

We were hopelessly spoiled. Friends who'd come for dinner were stunned. You eat like this *every* night? She rarely let me help her in the kitchen, which meant I didn't even have to do dishes. Of course, I never did my own laundry either. Remember the irritable young woman in the old TV commercial from the '60s? *Please Mother, I'd rather do it myself!* That would be me.

So what's it like going home? You can bet I still don't do the dishes or my own laundry. Try as I might before arriving, to promise myself I will be useful, that I will act like the grown-up person I've become and won't lapse into the old enforced passivity, it always happens.

Within twenty-four hours, maybe less, my resolve evaporates. Resolve? What's that? Who was I kidding? The reality of who I was living at home with my parents springs forth from deep within and that's who I am again. I'm convinced it comes from the cellular level. Deep in the molecules of my body is the person I have been buried in who I am today.

When Anne moved back home to live with her mother after the death of her son she did so for several reasons. On the surface, she and Charles were seeking the safety her mother's secure estate provided. They were feeling vulnerable and were still receiving threats from crackpots. Also, Anne felt emotionally protective of her mother. Elizabeth Morrow had lost her husband, her grandson, and her favorite daughter Elisabeth's health was now failing. Anne wanted to bring comfort to her mother and felt her presence and the new baby would help. But when adult children attempt to take care of their parents emotionally, it's a red flag: What she really wanted, but didn't know it, was for her mother to take care of *her*.

Unconsciously, Anne was looking for something she never got from her mother. She wasn't getting emotional support from Charles; he wasn't comfortable with his own feelings, so couldn't be there for her. So she did what many people disappointed in their marriages do— look homeward.

Of course, she didn't find it there either.

Her mother, ever the stoic, was caught up in her social causes and busier than ever. Anne, ashamed to admit her feelings to her mother, kept silent. The only release she found was writing in her diary, disappearing into the solitude of the grounds of the estate to cry where no one would hear her, and shrinking over to her own side of the bed at night to muffle her tears into silence in her pillow.

What should have been a period of mourning for her became an extended depression. The grief Anne suffered in the loss of her son was exacerbated by finding herself, once again, spiritually alone. The mother who wasn't there for her in her sadness wasn't ever really there for her. Overwhelmed by and immersed in abandonment, Anne mourned her son's and her own, past and present.

Thomas Wolfe was right. We can't go home again. Not if it means going back to where we grew up and looking to someone there to give us what we may have missed the first time around. The only person who can restore our losses is ourself. No one else can do it for us. Not our spouse, not our children, not even our parents.

We have to come to ourselves. We must face the reality of our own inner lives, to find our true shelter, the home that is within.

The Flow of Eternal Life

"It was a beautiful day, like spring...I felt a wonderful stream flowing through me that was this life—all this eternal life—going on, and it was joyful."

— LOCKED ROOMS AND OPEN DOORS, p. 23

A year had passed since the kidnapping and death of her son. Anne and Charles had just returned home from a ten-day road trip to visit family in the Midwest. The trip was exhilarating for both of them; they traveled incognito and were unrecognized the entire way. Lack of privacy had always been a burden, but it became increasingly painful after their son's death. After all, their fame had made them a target for the crime. Anne was elated to discover that there was some escape from the relentlessness of being spotted wherever they went. She was also happy to get home to her new son after ten days and she reveled in spending time with him.

One day not long after their return, she walked out-doors into the woods and found a log to sit on. As the sun warmed her she realized she hadn't felt so well in a long time. After months of feeling that nothing would ever go right again, she felt a glimmer of hope, a renewed desire to go on, and belief that the future would hold good things.

Anne thought back to the spring before, when she'd walked with little Charles over the small brook on their property and sat in the sunshine with him, filled with the pure joy that nothing else really mattered compared to this moment of deep maternal happiness and satisfaction.

Now, a year later, baby Charles was gone and yet she was somehow, miraculously almost, able to reconnect with the same feeling. She felt as if spring had returned the essence of that moment to her—and the essence of her son. The hope, the joy that surged through her now was like a positive stream that flowed through her body. It was palpable—beyond a thought or an idea—it was physical. It seemed to come from the outside, but it flowed *through* her.

Anne came to understand her experience of this "stream" as the presence of God. In a later work, *Dearly Beloved*, she talked about a stream of compassion: "...when you are in it...it feeds you and you give from it."[19] It was the intersection of the human and the eternal: God is here, concrete, in the details of our lives, but also outside and beyond.

Anne found herself in the stream for this reason: her trip. This mundane, earthy experience of being on the road alone with her husband, motoring across Pennsylvania, Ohio, Indiana, and Michigan, away from the frenetic pull of her mother's world and outside the gaze of a watching world was a crack through the wall of despair that pulled her down. She felt a trickle of hope now, the hope that she could have a future with some freedom. As she sat on the log in the spring sunshine, this trickle bubbled into a flow, and then a steady stream. It was a transfusion from death back into life. As this positive stream, this spirit of hope, surged through her, she was struck with the awareness that all is held there. She is. Her life and those she loves. Her lost son. The crime that took him. All that doesn't make sense; that is beyond her ability to take in and understand. Good. Evil. Everything.

I love the stream as a metaphor for God. It is living, moving, changing: sometimes gentle, occasionally angry; it is something to be experienced, not talked about. You don't sit down next to a stream or a river and analyze it to know it. No. You must get into it—experience it and feel it—to know what it is.

When I was a little girl, my grandmother planted this image in my consciousness, unaware, perhaps of the gift she was giving me. My mother's mother—Bebe, we called her—would alternately take my two older brothers and me for time alone just with her. These would involve dinners out at restaurants, movies, and sleepovers. She adored us and we adored her, so these were very big occasions.

But when it was my turn and it was time to go to sleep, I couldn't. Sleeping in an unfamiliar bed has always been a challenge. I remember lying wide-awake next to Bebe in her large double bed and hearing her soft rhythmic breathing. She was asleep. I wasn't. And it was lonely.

"Bebe?" I'd whisper to her. "I can't sleep."

She'd wake up and talk to me. She never got mad about my waking her up.

"Whenever I can't sleep," she'd say, "this is what I do. I close my eyes and lie on my back and pretend I'm floating down a river. A beautiful, gentle river. There are green trees hanging overhead and the current holds me up and just carries me right along. Try it."

I did. And I'd fall asleep. No small thing for me.

No doubt it was the combination of her love for a little girl awake and anxious in the night and her gift of a deeply spiritual image for me to practice that enabled me to relax and give in to sleep. I think of it as one of my earliest recollections of the stream of compassion:

the presence of God through my grandmother's love and this spiritual image.

As I grew up, my spiritual journey took me down paths that emphasized beliefs and intellectual understanding. Today, though, I have come full circle, returning to the image my grandmother gave me as a child. What is real to me is God as a positive stream of compassion that fills me with hope and energizes me to be myself and give out of that. I find I am "in the stream"—feeling most connected with God, others, my place in the world—when I am connected with myself. When, like Anne in the woods in the spring sunshine, I pause to reflect and feel what is really going on inside—when I am present to myself and compassionate with myself—I find the door opens to the stream of life. And it fills me with strength and love, and a current of hope, just as Bebe promised, that "carries me right along."

Red Shoes and the Search for Self

"I bought a pair of red shoes the day the airmail business blew up. They help a lot."
— LOCKED ROOMS AND OPEN DOORS, p. 190

Charles Lindbergh raised a public protest when, in 1934, President Franklin D. Roosevelt canceled all domestic commercial airmail contracts and directed the Army to fly the mail. Foreshadowing his future controversial involvement in the pre-war isolationist movement, Charles's involvement worried Anne.

And so, like any self-respecting woman, she promptly went out and bought herself a new pair of shoes. But not just any shoes. Red shoes. And she found comfort and temporary relief from her fears.

What woman can't relate to that? The urge to shop—to consume—is powerful; and never more so than when something else in our lives isn't going well or is beyond our control to repair.

How many times have I found myself splurging on something I hadn't planned on buying myself—something I hadn't really needed? A new piece of jewelry, a dress for which I really didn't have an occasion but perhaps would someday, a new purse when the one I'm using right now is perfectly fine. My son just shakes his head when I bring home a new pair of shoes, "You've got so many you never wear, Mom." It's a mystery to an eleven-year-old who finds sneakers and hiking boots perfectly adequate for all occasions. But I'm used to the chiding. I got it from his father, and my own father before that. What? What do you possibly need *another* pair of shoes for?

I suspect that even men are susceptible to the same urge to consume. I've seen it in the men I know in their conspicuous consumption of toys, from little boy toys like Legos to the expensive grown-up ones: the latest technology, cars, golf clubs. They have their red shoes, too. I think we all do.

It's because there's a spiritual drive behind consumption. Down deep inside us, below the simple pleasure of just enjoying things—it quells, temporarily, our inner restlessness and self-doubts. Because acquiring red shoes is acquiring hope. What hope? The hope that somehow, the red shoes will make all the difference. The red shoes are a symbol for what I want but don't yet have. The self I want to be, the life that's there but just beyond my reach.

Walker Percy writes of this phenomenon with astonishing insight in his parody, *Lost in the Cosmos: The Last Self-Help Book*. Having a new something, be it a dress, a hat, a car, is clothing our emptiness with something that appears to offer us something substantial: something not us, something that will fill our emptiness and make us something. Over time, though, the new something gradually is consumed and becomes absorbed into one's familiarity and selfhood. It loses the sparkle, the promise of something more.

What does a woman mean when she says, "I don't have a thing to wear," when in fact she has a closet full of clothes? While her statement seems absurd to her husband or a connivance to get more clothes, she is telling the truth. She does not have a thing to wear because all the things hanging in her closet have been emptied out and become invisible.[20]

I know this to be true. What's the difference between a new dress hanging in my closet with the price tag still on and a dress I've worn for several years and tired of? It's the difference between promise and either neutrality or outright revulsion. What, that old thing? Ugh. Did I actually ever *wear* that?

Over lunch with a friend recently we discussed actress Juliette Binoche's clothes in the film *Chocolat*. Belying her true identify, a vagabond angel who moved with her young daughter from village to village in 1950s France, Juliette's character dressed like a sophisticated Parisienne woman down to her shoes, which were high heels. Red ones. No matter that the streets of her village were cobblestone. That wasn't going to stop her from dressing like a grown-up woman. My friend spoke of how taken she was with Juliette's red shoes, so much, in fact, that when she ran across a pair of bright blue heels at a thrift shop recently, she scooped them up. We both smiled. I understood just how she felt. And I know Anne would, too.

When I find myself shopping for "red shoes" I'm learning to pause and ask myself, *What is it that you're really yearning for? What part of you has yet to find expression or satisfaction in your life?* I find that these deeper longings are usually at the bottom of my desires. That doesn't necessarily mean I don't go ahead with the red shoes. Sometimes I do. There is some temporary satisfaction there—but it is temporary. Finding the self "that's just beyond my reach" requires not reaching out for something external, but reaching down deeply inside and having the courage to release what is already there.

Reading to Know
You're Not Alone

"I would rather sit and read...than do anything else—even in the morning (there's something wicked about reading a novel in the morning). I can't put it down. I can't remember when I felt that way about a book."

⟶ LOCKED ROOMS AND OPEN DOORS, pp. 196-197

Anne wrote her sister Elisabeth from St. Louis, where she and Charles stayed for several days while they waited for the new plane that was being built for them. The plane took longer than expected and Anne was looking for ways to fill her time.

At the age of twenty-eight she was reading *War and Peace* for the first time. She confided to her sister that she was swept up in the romanticism—Prince Andrey, the court balls, the duels! A bit sheepishly, she admitted she felt she was a little old to be so taken with the romance of it all, that she should probably have read it years ago. But the fact is she was taken with it.

Great fiction, to me, is something of a miracle. Out of the inner world of the author springs a creation. The world she creates has characters and things that happen to them, and you come to care about them in a way that makes you want to stay there, live with them for a while, and see how things come out. And if the author's really done her job, you don't want it to end. You want that world to go on and on.

I know the pull of the novel Anne describes. How a story can so grab your attention that everything that's real and three dimensional around you pales and you are drawn into the imagination of the author to the exclusion of everything else. How the world of the story can be so compelling that it supersedes the normal routines of daily life. Dishes pile up, laundry sits, things that normally get your attention don't seem so important.

I have to agree with Anne—is there anything so delicious as reading a novel *in the morning*? No doubt, it's our Puritan heritage that makes it seem wicked, since morning is typically a time of heightened productivity for most Americans. There are even some who consider reading for pleasure at all to be self-indulgent—something you should allow yourself only when on vacation.

I find it helpful to ignore all this guilt. Even during my busiest times, if I don't have a novel on my bedside table I'm currently in the midst of, I feel deprived.

My friend Carol called in sick once so she could stay home to finish a novel. She was in the middle of Chaim Potok's *Davita's Harp*. The story absolutely gripped her, and she was not about to let anything get in the way of this experience. Not even her employer. I've always admired her for that. There was something in the character Davita's struggle with parental heritage, religious identity, and artistic expression that mirrors what has been and remains important for Carol. It's been more than ten years since she read it, but she can still discuss Davita's story as if it had happened to someone she knew well.

A wise man once said, "We read to know we are not alone." When you pick up a novel and read, you enter into the inner world of the author. If the author has not written out of himself, you too will find the book an escape from yourself. (There's plenty of that kind of writing around. You might as well just watch television.) But if the author has written an honest book—out of her own deepest self—you find yourself there, because underneath it all, we are really much the same. We all want to love and be loved, we all want to find meaning and our own place in the world. A communion occurs between you and the characters in the story and, although you are not part of the story, you enter in. You come to care for the characters because in them you find yourself. Their hopes, dreams, struggles, losses, and triumphs are yours. Two inner worlds connect—the author's and yours—and you find you are not alone. You find you are more connected to others in your common humanity than you'd realized.

When, like Anne, I find a book that I just can't put down, I rejoice. To give myself over to the power of a story is more than a luxury. As I enter into the inner world of another I find that—far from escaping it—I experience my own life, in some mysterious, perhaps unconscious way, even more deeply.

Comfort for the Body is Comfort for the Spirit

"I should take all these things and many others—small and big physical pleasures—take them for what they are in themselves. Hot baths and eau de cologne on one's body, and the heat pad at one's feet at night. And things to eat, too, toast and sherry—take them and use them deliberately, fiercely."

⎯⎯ LOCKED ROOMS AND OPEN DOORS, p. 213

The year after the kidnapping and death of Anne's infant son was difficult for her. Grieving the loss of her child, returning home with her husband to live with her mother, and trying to write her first book, Anne was weighed down with despair. In the midst of her depression she managed to find a measure of solace. She discovered that small luxuries that comfort the body helped.

This was a revelation for a woman raised in a family steeped in Presbyterian Calvinism, where things of the body were subjugated to the life of the mind and separated from the life of the spirit. In this world, relishing the senses was selfish indulgence. These luxuries were available, of course; after all, Anne's parents were wealthy and enjoyed the privileges that afforded, but *not too much*. So for Anne to "deliberately, fiercely" embrace pleasure was a dramatic departure from her upbringing.

Today we'd call Anne's unabashed immersion in creature comforts self care. For my generation, this is common practice. We work out, we get manicures, we get pedicures, we read self-help books, we have massages, we eat comfort foods, we burn scented candles, we keep potpourri around, we use scented bath products, we drink specialty coffee—the list could go on. What's behind this? Some might say it's the overwhelming narcissism of the baby-boomer generation, the commercialization of our vanity. Maybe. But maybe not.

I think there's something about Anne's experience that, when stripped to its fundamentals, reveals something about the deeper meaning of physical pleasure and the role it can play. She's in a state of spiritual hopelessness when she discovers the relief of small pleasures. Sad, empty, overwhelmed by loss, and engulfed by the fear that nothing will go right again, Anne sat by the fire at night, basking in its warmth, and sipping sherry from oh, probably a Waterford crystal sherry glass that sparkled in the firelight. The glow of the amber-colored liquid in a glass that shone like diamonds, the slight pungency of it as it slid down her throat and warmed her from the inside—these sensations reminded her there was beauty and goodness outside of herself and that her body recognized it, tasted it, and saw it.

If you haven't known depression, it may be hard to imagine the pain, grayness, and deadness you feel. Your body, your mind, your feelings all are one, and they are flat, void of energy, lifeless. When you can take something in physically that causes the slightest ripple across the flatness, that stirs even the tiniest wave of pleasure, your body registers that to your mind and your feelings: it's life! Here is something that feels good; there *is* goodness out there that I can apprehend. A glimmer of hope, a reminder.

Our generation's obsession with self care isn't simply an indication of the superficial materialism of our culture. Instead, it reveals our spiritual hunger, our unrecognized despair, and our search for hope and meaning. In the movie "You've Got Mail," the Tom Hanks character, Joe Fox, describes what Starbucks coffee means for many Americans:

"The whole purpose of places like Starbucks is for people with no decision making ability whatsoever to make six decisions just to buy one cup of coffee. Short, tall, light, dark, caf, decaf, low-fat, non-fat, etc. So people who don't know what the hell they're doing or who on earth they are can—for only $2.95—get not just a cup of coffee, but an absolutely defining sense of self."[21]

Funny? Yes. Pathetic? Maybe. True? Absolutely. Joe Fox, arrogant and sarcastic as he may be, puts his finger on the state of our collective souls. We are cut off from ourselves and we long to be reconnected.

I know that after a workout I feel more alive. My body is awakened and my sense of vitality is heightened. I realize there is a direct link between my body and my spirit. I don't see them or experience them as separate, distinct entities the way I used to. There is some mysterious interconnection. And so I find, as Anne did, that being good to my body, taking care of it, enjoying it, and relishing its pleasures, feeds my spirit, strengthens me, and nudges me toward hope.

Love and the Stream of Compassion

"Love is a force in you that enables you to give other things. It is the motivating power. It enables you to give strength and power and freedom and peace to another person...It is a power like money or steam or electricity. It is valueless unless you can give something else by means of it."

— LOCKED ROOMS AND OPEN DOORS, p. 231

Anne's thought on what love really is came on the heels of a stimulating conversation she had with Margot Loines, the woman who would later marry her brother. Even as a young woman Anne began to understand that love is not an entity that you can give: "...like an armful of flowers. And a lot of people give love like that—just dump it down on you, a useless strong-scented burden."[22] Rather, it is a power, a flow that energizes you to give other things *out of it*.

I think this is profoundly true. More and more I see that love is not this thing that I possess, that I hand over like I would a Hallmark card. It is something I am inside of, that I give out of. Instead of "I give you my love," it's "All that I do toward you comes out of this force inside me."

It reminds me of Anne's metaphor for God as the stream of compassion. When I am "in the stream," I love. All that I am, all that I do comes out of this place that flows through me. When I live out of this place, I can be a channel for love to flow through.

To be in the stream of compassion—to love—begins with me. I have to be present to myself, honest with myself, and compassionate and merciful to myself to open the door. And then I am free to love. The presence, honesty, and compassion that I give myself, I can give to another. It enables me to really see another person, empower them to be themselves, and to want the best for them. It doesn't feel hard to do this; it's not a burden or a sacrifice. It feels natural, as if it comes out of a flow inside me. *It is a power, like money or steam or electricity.* It's not sentimental and it's not always pretty. But it wants good and power and strength for the other.

I've experienced the difference between what it's like to live out of this place and not live out of this place most dramatically in my teaching life. I've taught elementary school students off and on for many years. It is one of the hardest jobs you can imagine. If you've ever planned and carried off a children's birthday party, think about doing that five days a week for six hours a day—only the activities you plan have to be meaningful and educational, keep the students involved, and get them ready for life. Not only that, children bring their emotional lives into the classroom and generally set them right out there on their desks. *Hel-lo! Here I am.* They don't have the ability to hide their emotional lives as adults do. So you're dealing with that as well. Exhausting, right? You get the picture.

I used to experience the responsibility of all this as crushing. I felt the weight of all of it—it felt like it was up to me to carry and solve all the problems and make everyone and everything okay.

It doesn't feel that way anymore.

When I analyze why, I see that as I get more in touch with myself and my inner life, I begin to see what is my responsibility and what isn't. I can't solve everyone's problems and fix everyone. I don't have that kind of power; no one does. And yet my good will has only increased. As I've grown to be more compassionate toward myself, I become naturally more compassionate toward others. It doesn't require effort. It just happens.

I've noticed a subtle yet noticeable difference in the way I teach. I'm better able to connect with my students when I'm connected with myself. I'm freer to share my real feelings with them. If I'm proud of them or pleased with them, I let them know. If they annoy me or make me angry, I let them know that, too. There's an honesty and goodwill that flows between us and I know it's because I'm more aware of myself than I've ever been. At the end of the year I'm always amazed and touched by the kinds of cards and notes they write me. They're full of love toward me and gratitude for all they've learned—and it's because they have felt loved and respected by me. The stream of compassion has flowed through our classroom. It hasn't been something I've had to reach for or will to happen. It's felt organic.

And so, I find Anne's ideas about love and the stream of compassion to be true. When we are in touch with ourselves and merciful to ourselves, we open ourselves to dwelling in a flow of energy that is greater than we are. "Love your neighbor as yourself" is more than a commandment; it's really the only way that can even happen.

Friendship for Life

"I suppose people who are part of your life as
you grow up, really part of your life—
especially during adolescence—are bound up
in you forever."

— LOCKED ROOMS AND OPEN DOORS, p. 261

Not long after her sister Elisabeth's death, Anne ran
into her cousin Jay at a dinner party. Although
she didn't fully explain their relationship, it's clear from
her diary entry that she and Jay and Elisabeth had been
very close as teenagers and that there had been an
estrangement. Despite the awkwardness of meeting him
for the first time in several years and feeling that he'd
become hardened and embittered, Anne recognized
underneath the boy she adored—then and now. She discovered inside herself an imprint that he had made
because he'd once been important to her. Now, seeing
him again, his "familiar much-loved face" filled that

place. It didn't matter that their lives had taken different directions. His essence was the same.

There is something powerful and deep about a connection with someone who "knew you when." Whether or not it's a relationship that continues to grow, it leaves an indelible and lasting imprint. I consider myself lucky to have a friendship from adolescence that has grown into the present.

Cheryl and I were best friends in high school, but our relationship actually started much earlier. Her parents and mine attended the same Episcopal Church when we were born just one month apart, and we were christened as infants on the same Sunday. Cheryl likes to tell the story about how the minister bumped her head on the baptismal font. As if *that* explained all her foibles and quirks. It could. But I think the significance of this event is more about how we were destined to be friends for life.

After the baptism we didn't hook up again until adolescence, where we segued from Girl Scouts and Job's Daughters into pretty hip-and-happening freshman at Lindbergh High School. (I was also destined to write this book because of my high school affiliation, you see.) We were hip-and-happening because Cheryl had an older brother, Marvin, who was at the center of the most popular group of juniors in school. (You'd think that with a name like Marvin that wouldn't be possible, but it's true.) Cheryl and I were both beginning to outgrow our middle-school geekiness. She looked like a cross between Susan Dey and Ali McGraw, and I am sorry to report that I resembled Marcia Brady. Marvin dubbed us "The Black Beauty and The Blond Bombshell." His friends flocked around, and we were amazed to find ourselves the center of all this male attention. Even girls in his junior class were nice to us. We felt special and chosen, and it was scary but thrilling.

We'd read all the Rosamond du Jardin adolescent fiction we could in junior high to prepare for just this moment, and we consulted it now in order to know how to behave. *Wait for Marcy*, *Marcy Catches Up*, *A Man for Marcy*, these were our guidebooks into dating and adolescence. We wrote pages-long notes to each other during class and passed them in the halls between classes. As soon as we got home, we were on the phone. For hours. We compared notes about everything. We sang. We listened to each other breathe. There was no event too insignificant to report. "Who did you see between 4th and 5th period?" "Did he say hi?" We traded clothes and traded advice on everything from the correct use of Clearasil to how to dress for our dates. Cheryl still hasn't forgiven me for the periwinkle hot pants she claims I made her wear to a Chicago concert. We wrote stories to each other about our lives using the "Marcy" formula, inserting ourselves and the dates we wanted to have into the story. In our stories we always wore strapless prom dresses that had netted skirts like Marcy's, flecked with scads and scads of silver stars. We thought we were very funny. I can still read those stories and notes today—of course I saved them—and laugh out loud. It's like we were living high school, but also outside of it making fun of ourselves at the same time.

We grew up, attended the same college but hung out with different friends, took different career paths, moved around and lived in different cities, married, divorced, but stayed in touch off and on through the years with birthday and Christmas cards, and occasional phone calls and visits. It wasn't until we were in our late thirties and on opposite coasts of the country, Cheryl in the East and I in the West, that we actually reconnected.

Today we're in touch a lot. Thank God for e-mail. Our e-mails read a lot, in fact, like our old high school notes. She still makes me laugh out loud. But we phone too. Take the other night. It was Friday night and I was home alone. I'd just finished my last day of school, my son was at his dad's and I was feeling slightly blue because of the emotional letdown I always feel at the end of the school year. I was also trying to decide what to do about a date for a party that was coming up that would have a live band. I wanted to go with someone to dance. I put on Don Henley's "All She Wants to Do is

Dance" and then I knew what I wanted to do. I'd call Cheryl. She'd understand. She might even have some advice.

It was 7 P.M. in California but 10 P.M. in Maryland, and she was already in bed. We compared notes on our pathetic lives. "Yeah," she said, "I was feeling sorry for myself, so I listened to some Don Henley music and then went to bed." I shrieked. Destiny again. Ever since Neil Young's *Harvest* album came out, we've been in amazing musical sync. We are, like, so on the same wavelength.

Later that night I got an invitation to a dinner party—in Beverly Hills no less—for the next night. Naturally, I e-mailed Cheryl: "So there I am in bed at 10 P.M. after an exciting evening of Seinfeld, an Elizabeth Berg novel, and a dinner of popcorn and diet Coke—not to mention a great, uplifting phone call with my new old best friend—when so-and-so phones to invite me to a dinner party...Yes, I realize I shouldn't be accepting a last-minute invitation like that—you know what *The Rules* girls would say..."

I treasure that I have a friend in my life that I can be silly and adolescent with. I don't have to always be my adult self with Cheryl. I can let her in on my insecurities, my longings and hopes, and the parts of myself that I don't generally reveal to most people. I can do this with her because along with our long history, we think the world of each other, and we let each other know it. And so, we are free to tease each other and be outrageously breezy; and we can be serious and intense too. Staying connected with Cheryl keeps me connected with that teenager I was so long ago, and I like that. I don't like to lose anyone—not even parts of myself.

The "imprint" that a person important to you when you're young makes that Anne talks about was created in each of us long ago. Cheryl might say it was from her bump on the head; I like to think it was destiny.

Trust Your Apathy

"I am beginning to respect the apathetic days. Perhaps they are a necessary pause: better to give in to them than to fight them at your desk hopelessly; then you lose both the day and your self-respect. Treat them as physical phenomena—casually—and obey them."

— LOCKED ROOMS AND OPEN DOORS, p. 276

love this advice. It so goes against the unspoken rule in our culture to grit your teeth and slog on, no matter what.

Feeling tired, sad, or depressed? Get over it. Better yet, take Prozac. And then get over it. At all costs, keep busy, keep moving, keep achieving. Don't slow down or you'll never get where you want to be. And the guy behind you will overtake you and get ahead of you.

Who can deny we are an externally motivated culture, taught from early on to move away from the feelings that connect us to our spirituality and inner voice?

Anne struggled with apathy around writing her first book after the kidnapping and death of her son. Her family legacy and that of her husband, Charles, was to suppress pain through action. All of them dealt with difficult feelings by moving away from them. Her parents were wrapped up in public service, and Charles literally moved away from his own grief by taking to the air. Anne was encouraged from all sides to put the loss of her baby behind her by busying herself writing her book.

But she knew that was not the answer.

Anne's lack of energy for writing, no doubt, was due to the loss of her child and her isolation in her grief. She couldn't share her sadness with the people closest to her in any meaningful way, and so she worked her feelings out by writing in her diary and confiding in her closest friends.

During this period Anne learned that she had to pay attention to her inner rhythms. For her, learning to go with one's internal energy flow was like sailing. You can't force a boat to go further into the wind than it can without losing momentum and your bearings. The only thing to do is give it its head. It will swing and swing and suddenly catch the wind, bite into it and go. You may have to tack back to get on course, but ultimately you get there more quickly. For Anne, the road to writing her book was through her grief. She couldn't step around it; she had to go through it.

I have often felt that if I lacked energy for doing something I needed or wanted to do it meant it would never be there. Whether it's the energy for doing something as important to me as writing this book or something as trivial as trimming trees in my yard, any lull in motivation meant the energy would be gone forever; the thing would never happen. I have come to see that energy for any particular thing, like so much in life, simply ebbs and flows. There may be obvious reasons for it—as in one's energy being tied up in grieving the loss of a loved one—or the reasons may be more mysterious. Maybe the time is just not right.

What is becoming clearer to me is that I can trust my internal inclinations. When I am impelled to do one thing and not another that may even appear to make more sense, I have learned to go with my impulse. When I do, I find, just as in Anne's sailing metaphor, that while the path may be less direct, I get to my goal more quickly. And I avoid the wasted doldrums of guilt and self-chastisement and "I should be doing such and such."

Recently I'd been sitting at my computer writing for four hours. I stopped for lunch and began to think about the things I needed to do in the afternoon: go to the bank, get the tires on the car rotated, exchange a scarf I needed for a wedding, stop at the grocery store. Yawn. I was exhausted from sitting and concentrating all morning and felt no desire to do all those things. Yet they needed to be done. I really wanted to get outside—it was a gorgeous, sunny eighty-degree day—and be in the water. And so I did. I went for a swim, dipped in the Jacuzzi, sunned for a while, and relaxed. Two hours later I was rested, showered, and able to do my errands easily. Had I pushed myself to do them first I would have felt tired, cranky, and put-upon. My little detour ended up being just the thing I needed to help me reach my goal.

A list of errands may be a small thing, but I find the principle holds true for the bigger things as well. When, like Anne, I "trust my apathy" and stop to consider what I really want and need in any moment, I hold life and life holds me much more graciously.

It's What You Don't Know About Yourself That Can Hurt You

"Your daily emotions are not important enough to warrant being written down, Amey thinks. Everyone has them, everyone goes through them, do not give so much weight to them. I think she is right...and yet I still think I must write out what I feel, otherwise there is too much stopped up in me. They become more important not written."
⁓ LOCKED ROOMS AND OPEN DOORS, p. 286

Anne's instincts were right, of course. And Amey, well meaning as she may have been, was wrong. Quite wrong. Amey, a good friend of Anne's mother, was, like her mother, immersed in a Calvinistic world-view of self-negation. In this conversation with Amey about keeping a diary, Anne was reminded of the message of her childhood: Deny the self, stamp out your longings, lose yourself in service to others. She gave intellectual assent to it because it was what she'd known all her life, but her heart told her it was false.

Anne was flooded with feeling after the kidnapping and murder of her son. She was surrounded by people who denied and ignored their feelings. Charles refused to talk about the tragedy and immersed himself in his work; her mother, still grieving her own husband, her first grandchild, and coming to terms with the failing health of her eldest daughter Elisabeth, threw herself into philanthropic work at a pace Anne found dizzying. Anne had nowhere to turn with her own feelings except her diary. Those closest to her were not only unavailable, but she felt they would judge her for being weak and self-indulgent.

Amey's diatribe was one more slap in the face Anne absorbed. But she continued to pour out her real feelings in her diary. Where else could she go?

Anne was right when she said feelings become more powerful when unexpressed. I find that my own unrecognized feelings control me. If I'm sad and don't give myself space to grieve, I become paralyzed, apathetic or empty. If I'm angry with someone and I don't know it or deal with it, my relationship with them is controlled by my anger. The anger will be there in every word I speak, every gesture, every interaction. It may be covert, but it will be there.

A few years ago I heard Maya Angelou speak, and while I remember little of her speech, what remains with me is a lyrical refrain she would sing at intervals, punctuating her remarks: "There's no hiding place down here...there's no hiding place down here..." This phrase from an old slave spiritual went right into my heart. The truth will out. There is no escaping yourself or your feelings, ultimately. You can run away from yourself, but as Anne says, "it just rears its head more terribly than ever."[23]

We run away from ourselves in so many ways. We work too much, lose ourselves in the lives of our spouse or children, watch too much TV, become a little too active in PTA or religious activities, drink, take drugs, work out fanatically, marry the wrong person, have an affair. Excess, I think, is the hallmark of escape. While some of these activities may look deceptively admirable from the outside, the core of self-abnegation is the same for all. And the end result is self-destruction.

Anne knew instinctively that striving for awareness is essential. As a wise friend of mine says, "It's what you *don't* know—about yourself—that can hurt you."[24] The choice to be numb to our feelings is a losing choice every time. There is always a cost. Remember, there's no hiding place down here.

Writing Through the Pit of Fear

"I realize the fear of this discouragement is what keeps me from starting to work... Perhaps I should accept it as part of the work, a perfectly normal stage that has to be faced and gone through—part of accomplishing anything—instead of something that is a great pit to be avoided. Perhaps the only road to accomplishment is right through the pit."

— LOCKED ROOMS AND OPEN DOORS, p. 317

Anne was just getting started on her second book, *Listen! the Wind*, the story of their exploratory trip around the North Atlantic. She pored over her diaries, letters, and pictures from the trip and the outlines and notes she'd made, but found only dead ends. Nothing seemed to have any meaning or life. But as I sought clues in her diary, I learned she was preoccupied with the coming war in Europe, and feeling that her efforts to write a travel book were trivial in the face of looming events.

Two days later she received a letter from Harold Nicolson, the British writer whom she had come to know when he had worked on a biography of her father. During that time he had recognized her talent and encouraged her early publishing efforts. In this letter he praised her first book and wrote optimistically about England's war posture. Encouraged, Anne returned to her work, bursting with new energy and ideas.

Anyone who does creative work is familiar with the pit. The dark slough has many faces: self-doubt, fear, panic, paralysis, apathy, meaninglessness. Where does the pit come from? How do you get around it? These are the questions writers always struggle with. Some create rituals for themselves to avoid it. I'm told Hemingway always stopped in the middle of something so he'd have a thread to pick up on and know where he was going when he came back. Isak Dinesen began her writing sessions by editing and rewriting her previous day's work. Alcohol is another way some writers deal with the pit— just camouflage it.

I tend to agree with Anne though. I don't think the pit is something to be avoided or managed, but rather, it's something to muck through. In fact, I think the most honest writing comes out of going through it. For what is the pit? It's our emotional life. The pit is not out there, after all. It's inside us.

I am convinced that every writer who is impassioned about his or her subject identifies at some deep level with that subject. Even the most objective biographer—-if there is such a thing—connects with his subject at an unconscious level. It's from this depth that intellectual interest springs. We long to understand the stories of others because whether we know it or not, we hope to learn something about ourselves from them.

When a writer tries to write honestly, she has to face her own feelings that the work stirs up. I had to do this recently when Anne Morrow Lindbergh passed away.

I came home from work on the evening of February 6, 2001, to a message on my answering machine. The voice was full of weight. I felt it physically before my mind understood. *What is it? Oh my God. That's it—she's gone. She is finally gone.* I had never met her, but when you come to know someone's writing well, you feel you know that person.

When I sat down to write a few days later, the words stuck. They hardly came at all. I reread something I'd written before and it fell flat. Meaningless. What I managed to eke out seemed false—as though the deepest part of me was inaccessible and I was working from another realm. What was real seemed beyond my reach then, and I finally gave up.

I put on some music and curled up on the sofa. James Taylor. The music reached inside and gently opened the door to what I was feeling. Fear and loneliness welled up and I knew then what I'd been avoiding the past few days. Suddenly I felt very young and vulnerable and alone.

Why was Anne's death triggering these feelings for me?

Because at some deep level I'd identified with her—the aloneness I recognized beneath her words was in me, too.

Because some place inside I didn't know that—despite her extraordinary self-awareness—she came to really understand her own aloneness and where it came from.

Because I suspect she died—despite being surrounded by her family—still feeling profoundly, inexplicably, spiritually alone.

And what did this mean for me?

I was afraid it could happen to me too.

And in the midst of this horrid state of feeling all this I sat down and—amazingly enough—was able to write. Once again. Right through the pit.

What happened to cause me to no longer feel divided and restless? The part of me, a young and frightened part of me, that wanted to walk—well, maybe run—away from getting further into this book because of how vulnerable it required me to be—had been seen and comforted. In moments like this when I recognize fear coming from a younger part of myself, I find it's almost as if my older self becomes a parent to this part of me. "It's okay," I assure the frightened child. "You're not alone. I am with you. I won't leave you."

And I won't. And that makes all the difference. When I stop and let the feelings in and let myself know where they come from—that's all it really takes. Then I can go on and do the thing I need and want to do.

Growth Underground

"She said too what I have learned lately, that when one is `vegetating' one is growing."
— LOCKED ROOMS AND OPEN DOORS, p. 374

Anne was visiting with an old family friend, Mrs. Neilson, the wife of William Allan Neilson, the president of Smith College. They discussed marriage, love, the importance of not separating the body and the spirit, having passion for work, and a German poet—Rainer Maria Rilke. It was a rich conversation for Anne who gleaned wisdom from Mrs. Neilson both in what she said and what she didn't say.

And she confirmed Anne's growing sense that even when she felt herself to be in a fallow period, she was still growing.

The past year had been difficult. The highly publicized trial of the man accused of kidnapping and murdering her child and the death of her sister, Elisabeth, rekindled Anne's grief. She struggled to be hopeful about the future and to move forward. She was ready to begin her second book but found it hard to settle in to work.

But she had a feeling that even though she seemed to be in a state of dormancy, below the surface her creativity and energy simmered. She was learning, and in due time this would be apparent.

She was right. Not long after Anne's conversation with Mrs. Neilson, she and Charles and their three-year-old son Jon moved to England. There she found relief from many pressures and painful reminders and settled in to a life of peace that enabled her to write her next book *Listen! the Wind*. It proved to be a richer, more complex book than her first. She had clearly grown.

Rainer Maria Rilke's work became increasingly important to Anne, both validating and shaping her understanding of her life and herself as an artist. In *Letters to a Young Poet*, Rilke wrote in 1903 what Anne came to know for herself:

Allow your judgments their own silent, undisturbed development, which like all progress, must come from deep within and cannot be forced or hastened. EVERYTHING is gestation and then birthing. To let each impression and each embryo of a feeling come to completion, entirely in itself, in the dark, in the unsayable, the unconscious, beyond the reach of one's own understanding, and with deep humility and patience to wait for the hour when a new clarity is born; this alone is what it means to live as an artist: in understanding as in creating.[25]

Anne came to see that she could trust whatever stage she was in. That even during times when she didn't feel herself to be flourishing and wasn't outwardly productive, below the surface, deep in her unconscious, life was brewing.

I know this too. When I was a seminary student I discovered Anne Morrow Lindbergh's work and became impassioned by it. I knew then that I wanted to write about her someday. I was far from ready to do it, but a deep desire was born then and continued to grow. Now, after a gestation period of nearly twenty years, I am writing a book I couldn't have conceived much less written then.

As much as we'd like to, we can't put our dreams on a schedule. "In this there is no measuring with time, a year doesn't matter, and ten years are nothing."[26] Did it ever seem like I might never write my book? Many times. The curves that life throws you often seem like obstacles between you and what you desire. But the reality is they are opportunities to take you further into yourself, into that deeper place Rilke speaks of that is the genesis for all our creativity and passion. Like the tree ripening in the spring, he says, we can stand confidently in the storms, unafraid that summer may not come afterward. Summer does come.

If we pay attention to what's happening in our inner lives and trust the wisdom that comes from there, fruit that we can see and touch will appear.

The Spiritual Value
of Possessions

"Aubrey to my apartment. He liked it and "saw" it. Now it is more real. He spoke about possessions, how beautiful possessions like silver, pictures, furniture, were tangible expressions of spiritual values you believed in. In a sense, then, they are creation, too."

LOCKED ROOMS AND OPEN DOORS, p. 331

Anne had just set up her own apartment in New York City, "a room of her own," where she hoped to find solitude and space for writing. She'd spent a good deal of time arranging her things, hanging pictures, and creating a place that felt comforting, familiar, and peaceful. When she stepped inside each day she was filled with happiness and a sense of security. Her brother-in-law, Aubrey, visited one day and recognized that what she had created there reflected who she was. The pictures she had hung, the books she had arranged, the placement of her desk and the things arranged on it, all revealed Anne's essence and her hopes for what she might do and be there. Aubrey's ability to recognize Anne in the room she had created confirmed her own perceptions. Another saw what she felt deeply about her apartment, and that made it feel even more real to her.

The space I live in has always mattered tremendously to me. As far back as I can remember, it's been important to me that my home was clean, uncluttered, calm, smoothed out, and filled with things that please my eyes. In my twenties I went through a period of internal struggle: that I put such high value on the "things" in my environment must mean that I am superficial, materialistic, or not socially conscious. These were all shameful things to be, particularly while I was living in the Princeton Seminary graduate school community where asceticism—read: *poverty*—was rampant, as was a theology of the mind that often seemed divorced from the material world and the body. Nonetheless, I carried on, caring always about my space simply for the sense of satisfaction it gave me.

During those days I began collecting Depression glass. There was a wonderful Depression glass store in nearby Lambertville, New Jersey. Nestled near the Delaware River, this tiny town was a favorite spot for Sunday brunch. After brunch I'd stroll the town, window-shopping and occasionally darting into a shop to check out an antique. I felt I'd hit gold when I stumbled on the Depression glass store one day. Here was an entire store filled with the colored glass manufactured and popular during the 1930s. Complete sets of milk glass, amber, green, ruby red, and cobalt blue glass dishes, glasses, pitchers, trays, and serving dishes. I felt transported to another era.

And so I began my collection of ruby red Depression glass dishes. I'd take them home and wash them in Dawn until they sparkled. They made me think of the candy apple deliciousness of Dorothy's ruby slippers as they gleamed against her powder blue anklets in "The Wizard of Oz." I'd set the vases on the windowsill and serve long leisurely brunches on the plates to my friends and pour countless cups of coffee into the delicate cups and saucers as sun poured through the window. The shafts of sunlight would sear through the ruby vases, and the brilliance of the red glass would burn as if on fire, bathing us in its glow. The light streaming through the transparent color filled me with a sense of well-being.

What the glass might have meant in the days of the Depression became real to me. I wondered if there was something spiritually significant about light and colored glass. My experience was that no matter how I felt, the sight of the light glowing through the scarlet glass filled me with hope. Is this why churches have stained glass?

Is there something behind this objective material thing that bears witness to a deeper reality? I suspect there is.

I continue to enjoy my ruby red glass, but I don't bring it out as often as I did in those days. Today it's the cobalt blue glass that has my attention and lines my kitchen window in my home in California. The sight of the deep blue glass in the window set against the emerald green of the backyard and the purple and yellow pansies and blue lobelia in the pots on the patio fills me with peace. There is something deeply satisfying and centering about this vision for me. As Anne suggests, the way we put our physical possessions together *is* a kind of creation—a mirror, in fact, of our inner space and the values we hold.

Our Legacy to Our Children

"...everything that I am trying to live and be and do is nothing if I cannot somehow give it to Jon."

⟶ THE FLOWER AND THE NETTLE, p. 73

Anne sank into domestic peace living in the rambling old country house called Long Barn just outside of London before the war. Having fled the United States with Charles and their three-year-old son, Jon, Anne had not only escaped unrelenting publicity and fear for the safety of her son but, for the first time was living independently of her mother. Having lived at Next Day Hill off and on ever since they married seven years before, Charles and Anne were finally able to establish a household that reflected them, their values, and their pace of life.

Her life at Long Barn was deeply satisfying to her. Fortunate to have household help, Anne was free to travel with her husband throughout Europe. At home she worked at her writing and spent time with Jon. As she immersed herself in the rhythm of her own life in the beauty of the English countryside, finally free of the pressures she felt in the States, her awareness of what was most important to her became clearer.

Jon's birth came on the heels of the tragic death of his older brother and he felt the aftershocks of this emotional trauma in his earliest years. That his parents chose to live with Anne's mother didn't help. During Jon's first years his mother was tense and depressed and his father immersed himself in activity. Jon felt it all and Anne worried about him.

But later, seeing him blooming in the English countryside and enjoying the benefits of the peace they all felt, she was more aware than ever of how much she wanted for him, how much she wanted to give him. And she realized that her life and everything about it—her work, her relationship with her husband, her time spent with Jon himself, everything—was her legacy to him.

I think this is true for all parents. Not only everything we do—but everything we are—is what we bequeath to them.

Often in our tendency to compartmentalize our lives, to separate what we do and its impact, we tend to think that it's only the things that we consciously try to instill that impact them, and that what we do in the rest of our lives apart from them doesn't really matter.

But it does. I'm realizing, with much fear and trembling, that everything about me—from my actions on the outside to the deepest truths about me on the inside—are both consciously and unconsciously taken in and registered by my child.

Children have the most refined and accurate sense of emotional radar imaginable. While they may be incapable of articulating or understanding everything cognitively, they know the truth about their world emotionally, deep inside their bodies. Regardless of what adults may say or do to protect children from what is true, they always know better viscerally.

With still more fear and trembling, I realize the power I have as a parent to shape and define my child's view of the world.

As parents we define the world psychologically for our children. *We are the world for our children.* Who we are determines the way they will grow up to view it. Is it a place that's loving, accepting, full of hope and possibilities for how you can take your place there? Or is it negating, rejecting, and without meaning or a place for you? The way that I see myself consciously and unconsciously—and the way that I treat myself—is what my child will inherit and ultimately come to believe about himself and his place in the world.

It's a deeply sobering thought to me, one that motivates me to try to cultivate awareness about all the parts of me, to not run away from the things that are difficult or painful, but to face them and work them out. The extent to which I am able to do this, I realize, is the extent to which my child will be free in the same way. Free to receive his mother's freedom and wholeness for himself as his rightful legacy, so that he doesn't end up having to confront any dark cupboards of mine that I was too frightened to face and clean out myself.

This is what children have to do if their parents don't do their emotional homework themselves. We pass our emotional reality along just as surely as we pass along our genes.

When I think of this I'm reminded of a passage in the book of Exodus. As Moses relays the Ten Commandments to the people, he warns them that the penalty for idolatry is that God will "punish children for the sins of their fathers to the third and fourth generation." While I used to take this quite literally—thinking this was pretty mean of God—the way I understand it now is it's another way of saying that if you put your trust in what is false—your defenses, let's say—then whatever internal gunk you don't deal with will automatically carry over for your children to deal with. And their children. It's just a fact. A law of nature. An inevitability.

I also think it's the reality the New Testament writer had in mind when he admonished people to "work out their salvation with fear and trembling." Face yourself. Turn on the light and see what's there. Be healed from whatever keeps you from being fully who you are.

However you think about it—whether religiously or psychologically or both—we know it's true. And it's true for all of us—even when the darkness isn't readily apparent.

A man who experiences a painful childhood and develops layers of defenses to cover his pain in order to live a functional adult life will live, nonetheless, to see the outcome of his choice not to face his deepest self in his children as they grow up. He may appear to be a model parent. When one of his children has problems that appear to come out of nowhere, people will scratch their heads and ask themselves, what went wrong? They seemed like such a nice family.

The darkness isn't always readily apparent.

Everything we do, everything we are is what we bequeath to our children. Does this mean we have to be perfect? That we have to be saints? No. It simply means our duty as parents—for the sake of our children and their future and their freedom—is to try to live as honestly as we can, to work out our own healing so we can be fully ourselves. Only then can our children be free to be fully who they were meant to be.

A Fertile Garden

"[A woman's life is] something wheel-like, with the essence of you at the center, reaching out on all sides in various directions. Of course there must be a concentrated core, a hub at the center that is specialized, in order to hold all those diverse spokes together. And each person must find her own specialized core."

— THE FLOWER AND THE NETTLE, p. 110

As Anne sank into the tranquility of the English countryside, and was finally free to create a structure and pace of life that worked for her as a wife, a mother, and a writer, she began to think deeply about what this meant for her.

She looked at other successful writers and was awed by the intensity and speed at which they worked, turning out book after book at an astonishing rate. For her to do so would require withdrawal from her family in amounts of time she was not willing to sacrifice.

It was important to Anne to continue to travel with Charles. One of the things that had bonded them from the beginning had been the way she so willingly plunged in to share in his travels and exploration. Now he was involved politically as well, investigating Germany's aviation military status and reporting back to government officials in America and England. In the midst of the precarious balance of peace in pre-war Europe, being present for him seemed more critical than ever. She also feared that their relationship would be diminished if she stopped sharing his work and interests with him as she always had.

Anne was aware too of how much Jon needed her and of how much she had to give to him. Together they relished their daily walks meandering through the fields of the English countryside. Anne tried to take advantage of this time to get in a little nature study—pointing out birds' nests, violets, and catkins, but she realized with some amusement that he had his own agenda: dead stumps. Jon loved their life at Long Barn. His spent his days exploring, dragging those stumps home, building a tree house with his father, and following Hook the gardener around and helping him. Seeing her son playing and learning and growing was deeply satisfying to Anne. Sometimes as she watched him through her study window as she tried to work, she would see opportunities to teach him or encourage him in some way. So she'd leave her desk and join him. She knew she had to seize these fleeting moments.

Being there for her husband and child could consume all of Anne's time and attention and energy. But she knew if she allowed that to happen she would be depleted. She would lose herself and have nothing left to give. And so she continued to write, continued to carve out time just for herself so that she could complete the manuscript for *Listen! the Wind.* There was something about this creative work—this relationship between her and her pen—that fed her soul and enlarged her. It was what made it possible for her to be the wife and mother and friend she wanted to be.

But it wasn't easy striking a balance. Her publisher was eager to see her manuscript, but Charles wanted her to join him on his trip to the Soviet Union. Jon's need for her, of course, was nearly constant. He would have liked her to be available every moment. Family and friends from the United States wanted to come and visit. People, relationships, and opportunities pulled at her from every direction.

The seeds of what would be Anne's magnum opus, *Gift From the Sea*, were germinated right there.

The origins of Anne's struggle to find a solution to how to remain whole in the midst of the demands of her life started to take shape there, in her peaceful English garden. She began to think out—to discuss with friends, to write out in letters, to sort out in the pages of her diary—just how a woman could hold onto a sense of herself when everything on the outside needed so much of her.

More than fifteen years later, at the height of the most demanding period of her domestic life as the mother of five, Anne began making trips to Florida alone. It was there on the beaches of Captiva Island that the ideas she had thought about, discussed, and written about began to emerge into a shape. The sea provided the inspiration that enabled her to access the wisdom that had gestated inside her.

The shells Anne collected as she walked along the beach provided the images she needed to describe the stages of a woman's life. Setting up housekeeping in the simple little beach house confirmed what she knew was the solution to her struggle to remain whole in the midst of life's demands. She needed solitude. To remain centered and hold onto herself no matter what centrifugal forces vied from the outside to deplete her, she had to actively cultivate aloneness and learn how to care for herself. Only in feeding her own spirit would she be fully herself and have anything to give. In this small book of beautifully crafted essays Anne gently named the problem of all women and offered a solution.

Elegant, wise, and profound, Anne's book is even more significant and revolutionary than it may at first appear. For what she had done in naming "the problem of woman" in the 1950s was to put her finger on the core spiritual problem of the twentieth-century—and now—the twenty-first century.

The dilemma Anne described—that we are alienated from ourselves and distracted and depleted by the complexity of our lives—is not only more relevant than ever today, but true of men as well as women. So too is her solution: Stop. Take some time away from the demands and busyness of your life. Pay attention to what is inside you. Find what it is that feeds you and restores you. Do that. Do it often. Take care of yourself first and you will tap into a wellspring that feeds you and enables you to go back to your life with authenticity and have something to give.

You can walk into almost any bookstore today and find *Gift From the Sea* in the religion or inspirational books section. It continues to make bestseller lists in religion-book publishing. While it is read mainly by women, I've know men who've read it and been struck by its relevance to them, too. It not only crosses gender lines but religious, political, social, and cultural boundaries as well.

In living so fully into the particularity of her own life—beginning in that quiet English countryside more than sixty years ago—Anne tapped a truth that is relevant to us all. And so in this intersection of the human and the eternal Anne produced not only a classic—but a transcendent book.

The Smallest Gesture
Reveals the Person

"...the essence of a person is as much to be
seen in a little act as in a big act. Everything
is a manifestation of them, if only you have the
intensity of perception to see it."

— THE FLOWER AND THE NETTLE, p. 110

Anne was rereading letters from Elisabeth. It had
been two years since she had died and this was the
first time Anne had dared to look at them. She had been
too frightened of coming up against the loss again, of
finding her presence and realizing the gap in her life
now that she was gone, of the grief that would be
unleashed. Delving into them was a shock. But not in
the way she expected.

Anne didn't find Elisabeth in her letters. Writing, she
realized, couldn't hold Elisabeth's essence. It was too
labored for her. Her brilliance was in her speech—

"direct, intuitive, and daring." It couldn't be captured on paper. The look of her handwriting—swift, delicate, nervous, and precise—reflected more of Elisabeth than her actual words did.

Anne was convinced that we reveal ourselves in the smallest, most insignificant ways. Everything we do, big and small, expresses who we are. She could identify her husband in the air by the way he flew his plane. The grace with which he banked the plane reminded her of the way he moved physically. His movement flowed easily. He flew the plane as though it were an extension of his body.

It's Maya Angelou's spiritual all over again: *There's no hiding place down here.* We reveal ourselves in everything we do. Anyone can be read—if only you have the intensity of perception to do so.

For our vacation one summer my son and I went on a cruise—one of those cruises that enable you to eat twenty-four hours a day if you wish. While other meals were low-key and casual, dinner was a formal occasion complete with dress code, linen tablecloths, nine pieces of silverware per place-setting—(my son counted the first night in disbelief)—and a menu from which you may choose from a fabulous assortment of offerings: appetizer, salad, main course, and dessert. Along with others at our table, we had a great time sampling our selections:

smoked salmon curled into the shape of a rose, duck, lamb, lobster, baked Alaska, chocolate mousse.

Our waiter, Martin, was courteous and prompt. Very prompt. In fact I was amazed at how quickly our food came to us. Almost as quickly as we finished and set down our forks, he whisked away the plates and delivered the next course. The service was wonderful but had a decidedly hurried feel. I noticed, but said nothing. But I admit I secretly missed the leisurely quality I usually feel when I'm dining this way. I wistfully noticed diners at other tables a course or so behind us, although we'd all been seated at the same time.

Martin's swift service gave him little time to linger and make small talk at the table. On the last night I tried to learn a little about him and his life. It turned out that this was to be his last voyage before his vacation. The next day he would be returning to Jamaica, to his family whom he hadn't seen in more than seven months. The longing to be gone, to be on his way, was written all over his face.

I now understood his serving style. It wasn't just about his efficiency, or even the fact that there were children at our table. He was hurrying each course along, because each one served and collected brought him that much closer to finishing his job, to packing his bags, and to going home.

Anne was wise in her observation. Who a person is—their essence—can be seen in all that they do, down to the smallest gesture. There is so much to understand about people, including ourselves—so much we *can* understand—if only we take the time and pay attention.

Hope For Old Age

"She comes out to meet you in the warmest and most heartening way. You feel that her life is full—that it was always full but that unlike most elderly widows...she does not live entirely in the past but is spiritually interested in the present and future too. It makes one not dread old age."

— THE FLOWER AND THE NETTLE, pp. 537-538

While visiting London before the war, Anne met Mrs. Yates Thompson for tea. The widow of Henry Yates Thompson, a barrister and book collector, Mrs. Yates Thompson was confined to a wheelchair and lived in a house "reeking with associations—pictures, books, whatnots, mementoes; another age." Despite being surrounded by reminders that most of this older woman's life is past, Anne didn't feel saddened or burdened for her. This was because Mrs. Yates Thompson wasn't preoccupied with her past or her disability. She was a woman who had learned to live in the present moment. So Anne found her to be spiritually alive, capable of being vitally interested in the world outside of herself.

This came as a surprise to Anne. I understand how she felt, as many of the elderly people I've known seem to shrink—not only in stature, but also in their ability to embrace the world.

But when you come across someone who is fully alive inside—the presenting persona: years, infirmity, fragility, their very closeness to mortality recede into the background—and the essence of the person is what you see.

I have been lucky enough to know someone like this. I count Georgenia as one of my dearest friends. She is in her eighties now and, despite intermittent illness, stays active and in touch. I tease her about being "in the know." If something interesting is going on around town, she is aware of it, and inevitably knows the people involved. She usually gets on the phone to clue *me* in.

I first met Georgenia more than ten years ago when, pregnant with my son, I moved to California with my then-husband. Her husband had retired some years before from the very graduate school position mine was assuming. As one faculty spouse to another, Georgenia took me under her wing, gave a luncheon for me, introduced me to other women in the community, and told me about activities she thought I might be interested in.

I thought she was wonderfully kind and thoughtful to reach out to this newcomer. We had a lovely, light, social connection. I learned over the years, though, that her kind of connecting was about more than just doing the gracious thing.

Not long after we moved to Claremont my husband and I separated. It was a scary, lonely time for me. A lot of our socializing had been with young faculty from my husband's school, and so many of my new acquaintances fell off abruptly. I assumed my association with Georgenia would too. After all, she and her husband were pillars of the graduate school community. But she didn't disappear.

That's when I learned she was a real friend. She entertained me at her home, invited me to talk if I wanted to, suggested I try a local support group for divorced people and offered to watch my son while I was there. When my brother died she called my friend Beverly, who was picking me up from the airport after his funeral. "Now be sure you're at the gate to meet her when she comes in," she admonished her. "Be sure you're *there*!" None of this "I'll meet you out at the curb" stuff for her.

Since those days our friendship has steadily grown. She still "baby-sits" Justin for me. More accurately he goes over to her home to spend time with them. She loves his company and he loves hers and her husband's. She and I go out to eat and go to lectures and art gallery openings—events that, more often than not, she's heard about. Georgenia always checks in to make sure we have plans during the holidays. She introduced me to a wonderful group of women who love books, The Betsy-Tacy Society, of which she became an honorary member because she was a friend and neighbor to author Maud Hart Lovelace in the '50s and '60s. Georgenia has achieved iconic status in the group not only because of this relationship, but because of who she is. The women revere her.

I revere her too. She shows me—as Mrs. Thompson showed a younger Anne—that old age needn't be dreaded. By remaining open to the present, our later years can be lived to the fullest in grace, humor, appreciation, and deep connection to others and the world around us.

How Intimacy is Possible

"[Connecting]...has nothing to do with speech
—quick brilliant speech—though one thinks it
has when one is young. 'Oh yes,' he says,
'mistrust always the quick and brilliant mind.'"
— WAR WITHIN AND WITHOUT, p. 30

Anne was deep in conversation with Antoine de
Saint-Exupéry. Upon meeting him she discovered
they had an astonishingly similar way of perceiving the
world. Both of them were connected to their inner lives
in a way few people are. Though they touched on many
subjects over the course of their visit together, this one
had to do with what was happening right then between
them. They were connecting. How did this happen?
What made it possible?

Saint-Exupéry said there were two kinds of people:
those you can talk to and those you can't. There is no
middle ground. Now this may seem like an awfully
black-and-white way of looking at human interaction,

especially for a poet-philosopher. But I think I know what he meant.

He went on to explain that the three greatest human beings he had ever met were illiterate. Two were Brittany fishermen and one was a farmer in Savoy. Real understanding, real connection between people, then—does *not* spring from the mind.

How many times have I been tripped up on this one? Too many. I am still learning to look beyond the externals—a person's words, philosophy or worldview, educational background, career status—to find who they really are underneath. Because there, I am beginning to figure out, is where connection happens.

I used to think that because a person had similar life or educational experiences as mine, or read the same books I have read, or shared opinions like mine, that connection was inevitable. But it's not. Like-mindedness isn't the basis for intimacy. It's something else.

Connection happens when the inner worlds of two people meet. This requires that both people are in touch with their own inner worlds, and that has to do with self-knowledge and emotion. Shared life experience, education, career choices, and opinions may draw people together—but none of these things automatically imply an ability to be intimate.

The truth is anyone can be in touch with their feelings and inner life; but few choose to because that necessitates not only embracing one's strengths but grappling with one's dark side as well. And true intimacy implies not only awareness of both but a willingness to own it and acknowledge it all as it impacts a relationship.

Saint-Exupéry warned, "Mistrust always the quick and brilliant mind."

He was talking about those people who have the language of truth, but are far from knowing the reality of it themselves. They may have the language of emotional availability, but their actions and behavior prove it's not real to them. They're usually very smart people, intellectually aware, but often sadly, very emotionally unaware when it comes to knowing themselves and their real feelings.

It's easy to be fooled by them.

You want so much for people to be who they seem to be. It's a huge disappointment and deeply hurtful when you've put your trust in someone whose words and actions don't turn out to be congruent. Of course, this is *all of us* at one time or another. We're all complicated and full of contradictions.

But this is the point at which connection can happen or not.

If we acknowledge our shadows, intimacy is possible. There can be a free exchange of the truth of who we are, acceptance, empathy, maybe even forgiveness if necessary, and connection. If we don't acknowledge our dark side, we inevitably throw up a wall, and closeness cannot happen.

At this point the relationship either screeches to a halt or there is an unspoken distancing; people settle for a superficial relationship where both tacitly agree not to get into the truth of their feelings. I have found this to be true for relationships with women as well as men.

I'm coming to see that every real relationship—friendship or love relationship—gets to this place. It's a moment of reckoning. If a relationship is heading toward closeness, it's inevitable. Two imperfect, complicated human beings are eventually going to bump into each other and step on each other's toes. When the icky, messy feelings come, as they always will, a decision has to be made.

Get into it? Or not? Face the less pretty parts of yourself and get through it to a new closeness that wasn't there before? Or put up a wall and deny the opportunity of deeper intimacy? *There are people you can connect with and people you can't.* It really is black-and-white.

Intimacy is a choice. Not that it's easy to acknowledge one's darker side. But the loss is great when you don't. And the rewards are unbelievably wonderful when you do.

Connection is not about having all the right words or a "quick and brilliant mind." It's simply about being willing to own and share who you really are.

Space to Breathe

"No American can understand the need for time—that is, simply space to breathe. If you have ten minutes to spare you should jam that full instead of leaving it—as space around your next ten minutes. How can anything ripen without those 'empty' ten minutes?"

— WAR WITHIN AND WITHOUT, p. 37

Anne and Charles had just returned from three years of living in England and France, where life had a decidedly less-driven quality. The pace of life was slower, less circumscribed by the clock, and leisure time was really that. As public figures, the Lindberghs had been granted privacy in a way they weren't in America. So it was a shock to Anne to return to a more frantic pace. Once back in America, the Lindberghs were besieged with people: requests for interviews, invitations to speak, invitations to social engagements. Many of these requests were appealing. Some were not. The reality is the Lindberghs had to say no to some things. And "no" Anne found, was not received easily by those who were asking.

This is no less true at the dawn of the 21st century than it was when Anne wrote it in her diary in 1939. The need for "space to breathe" is not widely embraced. While some may give intellectual assent to it: "Oh, yes, downtime—good for you—unplug—get away—healthy choice—yes, yes," few have the courage to live it out.

The truth is, in twenty-first century America most of us live plugged in to our pagers, our cell phones, our computers, and our schedules.

You see it in the businessman who takes the day off from work to go with his son on a school field trip. On the school bus he's constantly on his cell phone, checking in with the office, clients, and who knows who else. Here's his chance to connect with his son and he's yakking away—his body's there but his heart is somewhere else.

You see it too in the way we organize our children's lives. When my son was a baby my eyes were quickly opened to the way parents do it now. The busyness starts early. First there's Mommy and Me and Gymboree. Swim lessons. Preschool. Organized sports almost as soon as a child can stand and take directions. Play dates. Elementary school brings more. Music lessons, art lessons, more organized sports, and tutoring for getting that jump on the rest of your peers. Don't get me wrong.

My son has done a lot of these activities and a lot of it is good. What keeps me reeling, though, is that many parents I know have their children doing all of it—and all at once. There is a frantic, rushed quality about it. A deadly seriousness about it. Families leave the house at dawn and return at dark. Their car is where they have their time together while they shuttle back and forth, and homework is often done in the car.

Yeesh. When do kids just get a chance to be kids? When do they get to be bored? Learn to create something out of old cardboard boxes? Have time to lie around and dream?

The way we structure our children's lives says volumes about how we structure our own. We don't give ourselves time to lie around and dream either.

At the root of it all is anxiety. We're afraid to stop or slow down. If we don't keep moving, keep busy, we will be lost. We'll fall behind. Our children will be lost and they will fall behind. Americans are a competitive people. We find our worth by comparing ourselves to our neighbors. The Joneses have started their four-year-old son Mikey in T-Ball. What does this mean for my four-year-old? Maybe I need to sign him up for T-Ball, too. If I don't, Mikey will always have that edge, and my child may be left behind. And on and on and on.

We are anxious about falling behind, and we are anxious about facing ourselves. So we jam those empty spaces full. Our busyness reassures us that our lives are full and meaningful. It keeps our anxiety at bay. For now. But it's only a temporary reprieve.

Because the truth is we do need our ten minutes. Our space. Our time to rest and just be. We can't know who we are or how we feel without giving ourselves the time and space to let these things emerge from within. The Joneses can't give it to us. Our careers can't give it to us. And our children, proud as we are of them and all their activities, can't give it to us either.

We can only give it to ourselves.

I have learned to relish my ten minutes. In fact, my ten minutes often turn into more minutes than ten when I have the luxury to let them. I find that when I draw strict boundaries around my work, whether it's teaching or writing, and give myself the space I need to do whatever I feel I want to—read a book, see a movie, or just lie on the sofa and listen to music and *do nothing*—I am replenished from within and I can go back to my work or my parenting and be better than I would have been had I ignored my own needs.

I think of the Judeo-Christian tradition of enforced rest on the Sabbath and I wonder if the wisdom behind this command grew out of the understanding that people simply need time off from all work and responsibilities, that we need to proactively rest. I like to think so. I wonder what it would be like to take a whole day every week to put aside work as people who followed the strict letter of the law of the Sabbath did. As I'm experiencing the benefits of taking small amounts of time for myself, it's getting easier to imagine trying this. And more appealing too. Because, I'm learning, the "ripening" that Anne talks about just doesn't happen without these empty spaces.

Leap of Faith Inward

"How much faith one has got to have to do anything and how easily it melts away—how vulnerable it is! It is the worst torture, I think—or temptation—when people undermine your own inner faith. It is so much easier to have faith in other people's standards—so much safer."

— WAR WITHIN AND WITHOUT, pp. 145-146

Anne found herself pulled off-center just as she sent the manuscript of *The Wave of the Future* off to her publisher. She had written a small book, which she described as an articulation of the "moral argument for isolationism."[27] As America teetered on the brink of war in 1940, Anne was torn between the world of her husband and the world in which she was brought up. Anne understood the perspectives on both sides, but her own pacifism influenced by her husband's pragmatic philosophy resulted in a position separating her from her people: "the artists, the writers, the intellectuals, the sensitive, the idealistic."[28] She stood with her husband in believing America should stay out of the war, but it was an onerous stance.

The question of whether to get into the war was so highly charged that it became difficult if not impossible for many to tolerate opposing viewpoints. The growing rift between Anne and the people she'd grown up with and cared about was excruciating for her. That they would misperceive the man she married and misunderstand his position was painful as well. In order to explain this, she decided to write *The Wave of the Future*. She attempted to build a philosophical bridge between Charles's philosophy and her own, but in reality it was an emotional one. The impetus for the book grew out of her desire not to be separated from either world *emotionally*.

Anne felt she had to write the book. She knew it would be misunderstood; she knew she would be criticized. And yet she moved forward. Perhaps it was the only thing she could do upon finding herself in this untenable position. Just as she always did when emotionally charged issues presented themselves, Anne turned to writing to sort out her feelings.

Apart from the controversial nature of the work itself, the book reflects Anne's struggle with trusting herself and her own point of view. That lack of confidence—

and the need for reassurance—resonates today, especially with women.

How hard it can be to believe in yourself, in your own opinions, to trust that your voice is valid and worth hearing. How many of us grow up with a worldview and a set of opinions about everything from what kind of detergent to buy to what political candidate to vote for that we simply absorb from those around us—that is never challenged? And live out our lives in this way: always looking to something outside of ourselves for cues on how to think, how to behave, how to raise children, how to vote, how to dress, and on and on?

For those of us who didn't grow up being taught to trust ourselves, it is far easier to trust everyone else. There's safety in living a life that looks like everyone else's. But the safety comes at a price.

When we don't live out of who we truly are, we live a life that's a shadow of what it could be. The richness, the color, the depth, and the passion in who we are never comes to light, and our potential is lost. We may make fewer mistakes and lead a predictable life, but we also eclipse real growth and lose out on a wide range and depth of feeling and experience.

I know what Anne means about the vulnerability of one's inner faith—I can easily doubt myself and my instincts.

Yet, I'm also finding that my inner faith is like a muscle—the more I exercise it, the stronger it gets. The more I trust myself, the more I find I am trustworthy and that only I can make decisions that are right for me. It's a little like walking on the deck of a ship that's being tossed on the waves. When I get distracted by the opinions of others, or compare myself to others, or look to the example of others to guide me, I lose my footing, stumble, and find myself hanging on to anything that's within reach just to stay upright. It's not a pretty sight. But when I center back to myself and my own inclinations, I can step with confidence, knowing I can trust my footing. I can get through whatever storms come up with grace and balance. This is not to say that I disregard the advice of others. Not at all. But they are simply not definitive for me.

How hard it is to begin to trust yourself if you've never been encouraged to. The torn-apartness Anne experienced before the war illustrates the power that those closest to us can have over us when we aren't taught early on that it's not only acceptable but good to trust ourselves. Anne didn't feel free to draw her own conclusions about America's role in the war, because she was so accustomed to deferring to the powerful personalities of first, her parents, and then her husband.

This is no small thing. There is enormous emotional power behind a dynamic like this, not unlike a tidal wave.

To go against it, to detach emotionally from the personalities—the tidal wave—is to fear being set adrift. All alone at sea. And the thought of that can be unbearable.

But, once the choice is made to reckon by your inner compass, once you begin living out of that place—you find you are graciously met. Life and its possibilities open in a way they never could have if you hadn't taken the leap of faith.

Doorway to the Divine

"This winter I have made a positive effort to do what Meredith says is the task of all true women and artists, to see a `divinity in what the world deems gross material substance.` To live in and by `joy` in its Catholic sense."
— WAR WITHIN AND WITHOUT, p. 165

I n the winter of 1941 Anne was in the thick of the conflict of whether the United States should enter World War II. Charles was a leading spokesman for America First, an organization that worked toward keeping the country out of the war. Anne's sympathies were isolationist as well. Pearl Harbor was eight months off, and the nation was deeply divided. Their position set up an excruciating personal conflict. While the majority of the country was isolationist, most of Anne's family and friends were on the other side, urging America to get involved in the war in Europe. For Anne the conflict created a huge chasm that few of her relationships could bridge. Many friends fell away and even her family relationships were badly strained. As in the past during times of crisis, she found a way through by tapping her inner resources.

Anne looked for comfort in what was right before her. She found reassurance and warmth in everyday activities. Looking out her window, singing with her son Land, nursing baby Anne, her daily walks in the woods with Charles, skating with him and the children on the pond in the moonlight under the stars and the cold black night—these were the things that grounded her and gave her joy. In these everyday acts she found meaning and transcendence.

I remember when I first read about Brother Lawrence in his little book *Practicing the Presence of God.* He was the monk who wrote about experiencing God in the humble task of washing dishes. When I read this I thought, *yes—* this is true spirituality. In my own journey I'd run across so much that emphasized separating the spiritual from the mundane. The significance of the material world was minimized, if not vilified as something to be avoided, because it would take attention away from higher spiritual things. That never felt quite right to me.

Webster defines mundane as "commonplace, everyday, ordinary," but also as "the secular world as opposed to the church," and "of the world; worldly as distinguished from heavenly, spiritual."

I'm sorry, Mr. Webster, but I have to disagree with your latter definitions. The mundane, the material, the here and now, the stuff of our lives is—far from being opposed to authentic spirituality—the *doorway* to it. This is where God is present. When the ordinary is denied or diminished, our physical-emotional selves are diminished, too. Our souls are cut out of the picture and we are left with our heads—and then our spirituality becomes abstracted from our lives and intellectualized. Faith becomes mere beliefs, objective truths to be argued over, and dogma to be held onto for dear life because that's all you have. You can't trust what's inside you— that's always to be questioned as suspect—so you must rely on what's outside of you.

Practicing the presence of God, being open to the "stream of compassion that feeds the world,"[29] I'm learning, happens right in the midst of the mundane details of my life. It's in helping my son get ready for his first week away at summer camp, knowing that nurturing his independence will help him to trust himself and help him grow emotionally and spiritually. It's in shopping for fruits and vegetables at the local farmers' market, with the satisfaction that I can put the freshest, best tasting, and healthiest food on our table by buying directly from the farmers themselves. It's in taking a moment apart with a student in my class who's frustrated in his work because of a loss in his life, listening to him with empathy, and giving him space to vent his feelings so that he can let them go and move beyond them. It's in finding myself sleepless with stress when I've worked too hard, and being reminded that I have to balance work with play to live graciously.

In other words, it's in everything. "Catching joy on the wing"—a phrase Anne borrowed from William Blake—is about drinking up what life has to offer, finding goodness and meaning in what is right in front of you, no matter how seemingly trivial or even difficult, and finding yourself—because of your attentiveness to the ordinary and your openness to what it has to show you—held graciously, right in the midst of the stream of compassion.

All Vulnerability and Sweetness

"Around the house with a lantern to look at the sleeping children and put on an extra cover. The miser's hour for a mother—she looks at her gold and gloats over it!"

⟶ WAR WITHIN AND WITHOUT, p. 223

love this image of Anne. It was 1941 and Charles was away on a trip. She was alone with their three young children in their small rented cottage on Martha's Vineyard. I can imagine her creeping through the house late at night on her way to bed after she's written in her diary. She pulls the edges of a sweater draped over her shoulders closer to her throat against the evening chill with one hand while she holds a lantern with the other. The children will need extra cover.

As she spreads an extra blanket over each one she pauses to look at the face of each sleeping child: Jon. Land. Anne.

What is it about a sleeping child? There is nothing like it to a parent. For one thing, no matter what he or she was like during the day—he could have been the reincarnation of Dennis the Menace—all melts away and is forgotten. The sight of a child's face in slumber will do that. It is all vulnerability and sweetness.

My own son is eleven now and nearly as tall as I am. I am aware every day of how quickly he is growing up. But when I steal into his room for a last look at night and see his face resting in profile on his pillow, I am struck by how young he really is. Void of expression his features soften and remind me of the little face of not so long ago, emanating trust and innocence—and I realize that despite his rapid changes he has not been on this planet for very long at all.

Gazing at the face of my sleeping child is like time freezing for just a little bit. I get to behold, for a moment, the child he has been in the person he is becoming. Perhaps this is why Anne likens the experience to a miser gloating over his gold. Having lost a child, she knows the transitory nature of life.

Part of each of us, down deep, wishes we could hold onto our children and keep them young forever. We want to keep them close and safe. But we also know, down deep, that they will only be in our care for a time. They are a gift to us only temporarily. We treasure them, we let our hearts fill at the sight of them, we do all we can to enable them to blossom and grow. And then we open our hands and—when they are ready—we let them go.

The Soul of a Marriage

"It is strange, I can conceive of 'falling in love' over and over again. But 'marriage,' this richness of life itself, I cannot conceive of having again—or with anyone else. In this sense 'marriage' seems to me indissoluble."

⟶ WAR WITHIN AND WITHOUT, p. 255

Why did Anne choose to stay married to Charles Lindbergh?

With the publication of A. Scott Berg's Pulitzer Prize winning biography, *Lindbergh*, in 1998, the question begged an answer. Until Berg's book the reality of the Lindberghs' marriage from 1945 on had been a mystery to the public. Anne's published diaries ended with the war years when the family settled down permanently in Connecticut. Readers of her edited diaries might have guessed where the marriage was headed. Despite the love and loyalty that was clearly mutual, emotional distance was apparent.

Berg's book confirmed what some suspected. The post-war period brought further distance for the couple. After a miscarriage, Anne descended into another depression that impelled her, finally, to seek professional help. Because he had no interest in exploring his inner life himself, Charles couldn't and wouldn't tolerate Anne's doing so; he punished her by moving out of their bedroom. He also continued his incessant travel. Before the war he'd always taken her along, but as their family grew that became impossible, and Anne stayed behind, alone with the burdens of their domestic life. Anne found comfort in her friends and, eventually, in an affair.

Despite her efforts at inner exploration in psychotherapy, Anne's trajectory in this period was similar to Charles's. Each of them ran from the core conflict in the marriage: he through travel, she through her affair. When Anne ended the affair it was not because of resolution in the marriage, but rather her own resignation. Charles continued traveling, and he was absent as much as he was home. Anne believed Charles's restlessness grew out of his inability to deal with his unexpressed grief over the kidnapping and death of their first child. And she accepted this. But not without ambivalence.

Her final novel, *Dearly Beloved*, was her literary attempt to make sense of her decision. In a style pioneered by Virginia Woolf, Anne revealed the inner dialogue of her characters to her readers during their convergence around an event—a wedding. The voices of the disparate characters, men and women, all are reminiscent of Anne. Her own complexity and confusion were revealed in this cacophony of characters who, in the end are united, regardless of their frailties, failures, success, or happiness. The message is that despite our choices, despite our pain, ultimately, all is upheld by goodness. Moments of transcendence in which Anne apprehended "the stream"—the compassionate presence that holds all things together—are what I believe sustained her.

The character Frances, mother of the groom, a woman who'd chosen to stay in a marriage with an alcoholic, revealed the heart of Anne's dilemma:

> She only knew she must follow the direction of her growth, and yet, in following it she mustn't shatter the wholeness of life around her; that small universe she had created despite herself, husband, children, home. The moving toward truth, the rooted-here of life's wholeness: this was the uneasy balance she had to keep. The two forces were always in conflict: the journey forward, the standing fast; the passion for truth, and the instinct to love...She was the tree holding them all, Frances felt. How could she shake them loose, let them fall?[30]

Here was the pain of Anne's marriage. She could not fully be herself. The "moving toward truth"—becoming who she really was—and maintaining the "rooted-here of life's wholeness"—the structure of life she'd created with Charles—were in conflict.

Anne knew she would never have what she craved in her marriage: emotional intimacy. Charles would never change. And yet she would not dismantle the life they had together to seek it elsewhere.

I find this understandable. This was a couple bound together by rich history, both public and private. Anne was in her early twenties when she married him. They had six children together, and they endured the kidnapping and murder of one of them. They lived during a time when divorce was uncommon. They had been partners in so much. I can see why it was excruciating for Anne to think about dissolving it. No wonder she couldn't conceive of having it again—or with anyone else.

And yet. And yet. That decision meant that she had to accept living with her repressed feelings. Charles continued to leave her. He would go off again and again, seeming to show little regard for her needs. Berg presents a disturbing account of the later years of the marriage, with Charles depositing Anne in a primitive A-frame in Maui and taking off, leaving her to fend for herself with no electricity, telephone, or paved roads, battling flooding and vermin. One aches for her abandonment. Why did she put up with it?

The fact is Anne was used to it. The deep sense of isolation she felt in her marriage was not new to her. She'd grown up with it; it was familiar. One who has this profound sense of inner aloneness looks inevitably to the outward security that marriage provides. Because facing the depth of her emotional abandonment that predated Charles was too terrifying, Anne magnified the importance of the outer structure of her marriage. It was the web they'd created that held them and all of their children, the myriad realities that make up the life of a family. And those things are important. Terribly important.

But surely the soul of the marriage, the intimacy at the center is what the marriage really is. The emotional reality underneath is what is really passed along to one's children. You can't fool them by simply keeping the structure of marriage in place. Children always know the truth. The Lindbergh children were undoubtedly impacted by the shadows in their parents' marriage. All five experienced divorces of their own.

Anne's decision to stay in her marriage was fueled, no doubt, by many things: her love for Charles, their shared and irreplaceable history, their partnership in their writing, the desire to maintain an externally secure structure for their children, and probably also, the fear of more aloneness.

As their lives have been archetypical for us in so many ways, so too has their marriage. The early days of their marriage seen in photos splashed across the pages of newspapers and magazines—the evident bloom of young love, the romance of two young and attractive adventurers making aviation history across the globe—surely this was the storybook marriage we all admired and secretly longed for ourselves, wasn't it? Opposites attracted and they called further greatness out of each other. Anne became more active and adventurous; Charles became more reflective and found the writer within himself. So many good things came out of this union.

I would like for this to have been the final word. The end of the story. But it wasn't reality. They showed us that even our heroes have shadows. Even marriages that have strengths can have deep and dark recesses of pain that beg to be brought into the light of day to be healed.

I wish this had been the case with Charles and Anne Lindbergh, that they would have been able to apprehend the pain in the chasm of space they needed to create between themselves just to maintain the marriage.

Confronting the shadows in a marriage is not only difficult work, it's scary, because it requires facing the shadows within oneself. But intimacy simply isn't possible any other way.

The God Has Left the Temple

"For this is the mark of maturity—the degree to which one can go on making the oblations, performing the rite when—as St.-Ex. says—the God has left the temple. There are always times when the God is hidden. But one must go on through the motions even when one sees no sense in it—clean out the drawers, bathe the baby, copy the last chapter..."

⟶ WAR WITHIN AND WITHOUT, p. 317

I t was the first week of January, right after Christmas in 1943, and Anne was in a post-holiday slump. The holiday was complicated by sick children—young Anne and Scott had colds. The household staff bickered incessantly and two days after Christmas, two of them informed her they were quitting. Soon after, Charles took off on yet another trip. In the midst of juggling her household and trying to keep everyone comfortable and happy, Anne tried to work on her manuscript, *The Steep Ascent,* with the hope of finishing it by spring.

She found herself in a funk. Out of grace and out of sorts, the daily tasks before her, which she usually approached with joy, felt empty and burdensome. The flow and energy and rhythm of life she normally felt was missing.

From the outside it might seem that her circumstances were trivial. Everyone gets colds; what's the big deal? Not very many people have the luxury of even having household help, much less having to worry about them getting along. As for Charles going off again—well, he'd be back.

But I've noticed that these little glitches in the flow of life—in all their seeming insignificance and sometimes even *pettiness*—have a surprising power to derail us temporarily.

I had a day like that recently.

My beloved hairstylist retired. I'd been going to her for more than four years. She knew me, and she knew my hair. She knew what I needed, and she knew what my hair needed. I needed my space to just read magazines if I didn't feel like talking. This was okay with her. My hair, because it's so thick, needed her special cutting technique to keep it from overwhelming me—along with highlights in just the right places. She took care of me, and I tipped her generously. What we had together worked.

As every woman knows, this is a rare and beautiful thing. Having a person you can go to, put yourself and your hair in her hands, and sit back and trust that everything will come out okay.

I was in total denial about Janet's retirement until I showed up for my appointment with the woman to whom she referred me. All my anxieties surfaced. What if this person had had a fight with her boyfriend that morning and I came out looking like Sinead O'Connor? What if she turned me from a blond into a brunette? What if I had to wear a paper bag over my head for a week or two when we were finished? A new hairstylist, as every woman knows, is an unknown. You put your head in her hands, cross your fingers under that nylon cape, and hope for the best.

I am relieved to say it was not a disaster. It was actually okay. But it was different. And it was awkward. Starting with a new stylist is like starting to date again after your divorce. It's just icky, and it takes time to get used to it.

To top it off, my face broke out that day. Aack. And here I am in my forties. How could this be?

Suddenly I found myself derailed: I felt awkward, insecure, off-center, and out of sorts. Sitting down to write felt uncomfortable. I had nothing to say. I forgot to do an important errand I needed to do and had to run out at night to take care of it. Things that usually go smoothly for me, that sort of flow, felt sticky. I felt out of grace. My rhythm was off. The God had left the temple.

But why? I'm a big girl. Am I really this vain? (Probably.) But I suspect it was about more than just that.

The fact is the interruption in my routine triggered my vulnerability. Putting myself in the hands of a new hair stylist and breaking out with a_____ (I hate that word and I can't even bring myself to write it) brought up feelings from long ago. And from somewhere inside the grown-up, usually self-confident me emerged my vulnerable, younger, less secure self.

The one who in elementary school dreaded going to school on Monday after getting a Toni home permanent from her mother over the weekend. Who in junior high was shy about changing in a crowded girls' locker room into that horrible one-piece blue snap-up gym-suit the PE teachers made everyone wear. Who in high school wore Clearasil to bed at night as a precautionary meas- ure so that if anything was even *thinking* about erupting it would reconsider.

The new, the strange, the unfamiliar, the fear of exposure—these were not comfortable feelings then and still aren't now.

When it comes to the mundane details of life, it's much more comfortable for me when things stay the same. When they're predictable. When I've got things in place in my life I can count on. It's all because, I think, of what these seemingly trivial things represent.

"....ordinary things help—inconceivably. They are the security of the rhythmic pat your Mother gave you rocking you in her lap. They are the safety, the infinite safety and deliverance from terror, that you got as a child, lying in bed afraid of dark and just touching, ever so lightly, with an elbow or a knee, the older person sleeping with you....They are trivial-on-the-surface things that indicate great wells of security and faith and peace and the whole unconscious, hardly noticed, but infinitely precious structure of life."[31]

This last sentence is so true. That's it. The on-the-surface things in our lives symbolize our security. They fit together to create a web that holds us, that forms the stuff of our lives that we can take for granted—that is so in place that we don't even have to think about it.

So when one of these little bricks is shaken loose, is knocked out of place, we can't be unconscious anymore. We're reminded that the structure of our lives *is* vulnerable, that our lives are fragile—that things change.

And it can throw us off balance and cause us to lose our sense that all is well in the world.

But only temporarily. For as Anne says, as we grow older, as we mature—we go on anyway. It doesn't stop us. We continue living our lives, going through the motions, because we know that life is full of ebbs and flows. Over time we learn that in embracing our vulnerability when the unexpected happens—not denying it or running from it—our faith returns. And so does the God to the temple.

The Must of Mutuality in a Relationship

"That is the best kind of relationship, the kind in which one is both a giver and receiver. Not the kind in which one tries unsuccessfully to fill up a bottomless pit."

— WAR WITHIN AND WITHOUT, p. 395

While living near the Cranbrook Academy of Art in Bloomfield Hills, Michigan, Anne found a circle of friends that sustained her during the war years. Charles was away frequently, and Anne was delighted to discover this community of people like herself—artists and intellectuals—a stimulating group who shared common values with her. One of these, Janet de Coux, became not only her sculpting teacher, but her friend.

Anne discovered on their first meeting that she and Janet shared a similar religious view of art. Anne recognized she had much to learn from Janet. The sculpting studio was a new world for her. Janet encouraged her and recognized her success in grasping the fundamentals of sculpting. The relationship grew beyond that of teacher and student. Anne found that she had something to give Janet, too, for she was also an artist—a writer. And she understood something of what it meant to live the life of one. The two women shared conversations and began a friendship that stretched beyond the studio.

Their friendship was satisfying and energizing because it was mutual. Neither woman found herself doing all the giving, or all the listening, or all the supporting. Each woman came to the friendship and had something to give out of her own strength as well as out of her vulnerability. It was a relationship of equals.

I know I've had friendships that haven't been mutual. Often I'm the one doing all the listening, supporting, or accommodating. Sometimes this can be subtle, and hard to see at first. I've also had friendships that have been off-balance the other way—where I've felt I've been the one doing all the sharing with little coming back. Either way it's no good, ultimately.

When a relationship isn't mutual, I'm left with a feeling of being drained. Empty. There's no connecting.

When it is mutual, a friendship leaves me with a totally different feeling. Each of us is interested in the other's life. Sharing is a two-way street, and the quality and depth of it is similar. Each person's feelings and opinions are valued. And far from being draining, a relationship like this energizes me. That's what connection does. When two people meet and there's mutuality, each of us comes away feeling seen, understood, validated, and strengthened.

The friendship creates something greater than the sum of our parts. It reminds me of the loaves and fishes metaphor from the New Testament. Jesus took five loaves of bread and two fish, blessed them, and was able to feed numbers unimaginable, and had some left over. It's like that with friendship. We share whatever we have with each other, emotionally, and it's multiplied. As with Anne and Janet, each of us is strengthened, nourished, and replenished, so that we can continue giving to others in our lives.

More and more I'm learning to let go of relationships that aren't mutual. I find that just as mutual relationships create positive benefits in my life, one-sided ones do the opposite. They deplete me and force me to be dishonest, which affects other parts of my life. The cost to my spirit is too high. And life is too short for that.

The Heart is Slow to Learn

"It was this way with the [loss of] the baby and Elisabeth, I remember now. The heart will not take it in all at once; it rejects it, it has to be told—a fresh telling, a fresh shock, a fresh thrust over and over again. And each thrust is as sharp, as cruel as the first, because in between the heart rejects the realization, it disbelieves, and then it must be hurt all over again. How slow a heart is to learn, much slower than the mind. So stupid, so tenacious, so heedless of hurt."

— WAR WITHIN AND WITHOUT, p. 446

Anne had just learned that Antoine de Saint-Exupéry's plane was missing. After France had fallen to the Germans, the author-pilot had joined the French resistance in Africa. In 1944 his plane was lost while he flew a lone reconnaissance mission over southern France.

Saint-Exupéry's death had a tremendous impact on Anne. They'd met only once, but Anne felt a powerful connection with him. He could speak no English and her French was not fluent, but it was no barrier to their understanding: "...he spoke 'my language' better than anyone I have ever met, before or since."[32]

Anne felt, too, that she knew him through his books. Here was a man with a depth and sensibility so much like her own, something she'd never found anywhere else in anyone else. Like Anne, he had the eternal point of view: an ability to see the deeper reality of life that's hidden to so many of us. She'd written her last book, *The Steep Ascent*, knowing that if no one else understood the underlying truth of her story, he would.

She'd never felt this kind of spiritual kinship before. Not even with Charles. And now she felt terribly alone.

Anne wasn't alone physically, though; after all, she had Charles and her four children, all brimming with life. Her life was full in that respect. But spiritually, emotionally she was bereft. Saint-Exupéry had recognized the essence of who she was as well, through her writing—something no one else had ever done before.

There is nothing more emotionally powerful than being seen and understood by another. Anne was forever changed by that encounter.

His death was impossible for her to absorb.

Anne remembered getting the news, not long after

her own baby died, that a friend's husband had been killed. She'd wondered if the woman felt the shock of how quickly everyone else seemed to accept the death as a fact. Flowers arrived, telegrams, sympathy cards, and letters were sent immediately. These expressions of the reality of death roll in "...so easily, without a murmur or a protest, without one rebellious 'It cannot be,' when you cannot accept the realization yourself, when it is almost treason to."[33]

The more someone or something matters to us, the harder it is to accept the truth about them. Human beings—emotionally fragile creatures that we are—develop these ingenious shields to hold the truth of what's most important to us and about us at bay. Denial is simply part of how we manage to get by.

It's the reason we can know something intellectually but not emotionally.

It's why therapy is such slow, hard work. The conditions that lead us to seek help are usually rooted in situations that go back to the beginning of our lives. As we grow up we develop defenses—ways of coping—so that we can function. We go into therapy when we discover that the ways we've always coped don't work anymore. Getting help is often precipitated by a crisis: a divorce, a death or other loss, any major life change. We may understand quite well *intellectually* exactly how we got from Point A to Point B, but knowing it in our feelings—in our bodies, even—is a wholly other kind of knowing. And it's only in this kind of knowing that real change can take place.

This kind of knowing requires the slow—ever so slow—lowering of our defenses. We let a little bit of the truth in—a fresh recognition—and up come the defenses again. It's simply too hard, too painful. But time goes by and we let down and let in a little more. Another shock of recognition. Just as painful, maybe more so. Only as time goes on and this process of letting in a little more continues, we begin to feel clearer, stronger. The truth, as excruciating as it is, does set us free. It's a knowledge that goes way beyond our minds, permeating our bodies and our emotions, transforming the way we live.

"We have to be utterly broken before we can realize that it is impossible to better the truth. It is the truth we deny which so tenderly and forgivingly picks up the fragments and puts them together again."[34]

The heart *is* "stupid, tenacious, heedless of hurt." We shore up and hang onto our defenses for good reason. Pain is not fun. But as we begin to let ourselves know the truth of whatever it is that's been difficult to let in, we discover that it doesn't kill us. Down deep we always thought it would. That it would stop us completely. That we couldn't go on. No. Far from it. It's knowing a hard thing deeply—facing the truth—that enables us to go on, finally, and be free.

Lessons From the Journey

"...there is a divinity which places our heroes before us only for a short period that we may learn one special thing from them, and one only—at that special moment. They are not meant to be our oracles for life."

— WAR WITHIN AND WITHOUT, p. 98

While living in Paris just before the outbreak of the war in Europe, Charles commissioned a sculptor, Charles Despiau, to do a bust of Anne. From November of 1938 to April of 1939 Anne sat for Despiau at his studio. He was a "...nice little man," she observed in her diary on their first meeting, "...sensitive, neurotic, but quite simple and shy. I like him."[35] As the sittings continued, Anne observed the way he worked and was fascinated. Doing the bust took much longer than she would have expected, because Despiau worked as though he had all the time in the world. He seemed to enter another dimension, oblivious to time or pressure.

A bit seedy, complaining often of sleeplessness and exhaustion, and racked with a smoker's cough, Despiau seemed at first a pathetic figure. But once he began to work, an inner confidence took over, his external encumbrances receded, and he was immersed in his art—trusting both himself and the outcome.

Anne was touched by this transformation—both by the intensity of his focus and by the vision he was able to realize.

A few years later, Anne struggled with her own inability to focus on her writing. She was pregnant. Tired, and unable to transcend her physical, emotional, and mental lethargy, Anne remembered Despiau's words about trusting one's inner timetable: "If you have three moments of clear vision in a day it is enough!"[36] Creativity is a gift that can't be controlled or forced. One must simply give thanks when one is in the midst of its flow.

That's fine for those three minutes, Anne thought, but what, she wanted to know now, do you do for the *rest* of the day?

She wished she could meet him again—now that she better understood what he was about—and ask him questions. Surely he would have the answers she needed.

And then she realized the impossibility of this. Not that it might not actually happen. Only that he probably would not have what she sought.

Anne understood that we encounter people in our lives—mentors, teachers, role models, and heroes—at a time when we need to learn a particular truth they have to teach us. She learned from Despiau the truth that an artist must work according to his or her own inner timetable. Anne struggled to allow herself to do this. Her acute need to please left her prone to worry about living up to others' expectations. Her interlude with Despiau opened her eyes to see it might be possible for her to follow her own rhythm.

If she were granted the chance to see him again, to ask the questions, she suspected she might be disappointed. No doubt she would have been.

When we have a person like this in our life, our tendency is to idealize him or her. Because that person exemplifies a quality we ourselves lack but deeply desire, we assume that everything about that person is to be emulated. We over-identify.

This tendency comes to no good for two reasons. First, it's a mistake to idealize anyone. No one has all the answers. Everyone is made up of light and shadows, complexity, contradictions, imperfections, and flaws. It's part of being human. Second, mentors come into our lives, not to teach us to be *them*, but to open up some truth to us so that we can be more *ourselves*.

But, when we're young we want our heroes to be perfect.

I was a twenty-something looking for a role model when I first discovered Anne's writing. The women I'd known up to this point had either been totally oriented toward relationships, wanting to marry and have babies, exclusively assuming their roles as wives and mothers—or totally career-oriented, single-mindedly following a path that seemed to eclipse having a personal life. The Anne I discovered embraced both. Her life included her marriage and family as well as her own work. Clearly, it wasn't easy for her to achieve balance—the search for it would be the theme of *Gift From the Sea*. But she seemed to embody the kind of life I wanted—and she had an inner sensibility that resonated deeply with me.

No wonder I identified with her and idealized her.

Growing up changes that, though. As I matured and gradually began to understand more about myself, I came to understand my hero Anne in a more realistic light too. She wasn't perfect. She wasn't the Ideal Woman with the Ideal Marriage and Ideal Career. When you begin to grow up you realize no one is. But that doesn't mean you can't take lessons from their journey.

The lessons I take from the journey of Anne Morrow Lindbergh are many. But the one thing, the special thing that I believe I was meant to learn from her is simply this: Pay attention to your inner life. It is the source of who you are, what you can be, and what you have to give. Just as my grandmother's first-edition copy of *Gift*

From the Sea sat on that bookshelf waiting for me all those years—so too are many of the gifts each of us already possess. Waiting to be opened, waiting to be read, waiting to be claimed. When we are ready.

ANNE'S LEGACY
The Journey Not the Arrival

By the end of the 1940s the tumult of the war years was over, and Anne was immersed in her life in suburban Connecticut as a wife and mother of five children. She had wrestled personally and intellectually for years with the issue of how women reconcile and balance the parts of their lives: selves, husbands, children, and careers. But it wasn't until she was in the midst of the full demands of a large family life in the 1950s that her ideas came to fruition in *Gift From the Sea*.

Anne's central insight, that attention to one's inner life is the key to fulfillment and balance, was quietly revolutionary. The claim that women must make time for themselves radically went against the fifties' notion of the good woman as one who sacrifices all—including herself—for others. Anne's message is timeless. Even though the patterns of women's lives have evolved dramatically since that decade, many women still struggle with whether they have a right to create a space for themselves in their lives. Anne Morrow Lindbergh convinced us that it's essential.

The next two decades brought change. Children grew up and left home, Charles became active on behalf of conservation, they traveled widely and established homes in Switzerland and Maui, and Anne continued to write and publish. Her work included a volume of poetry called *The Unicorn*, two essays on celestial and terrestrial exploration in *Earth Shine*, and a novel, *Dearly Beloved*, which explored marriage from a variety of perspectives and stages in life. Most significant was Anne's decision to publish five volumes of her diaries and letters, a task that would consume her time and energy for several years.

The irony of this intensely private person publishing such personal writing can be explained by Anne's deep desire to be truly seen. Rooted in her childhood experience, her sense of being misunderstood was played out in her adult life. Both Anne and Charles chafed for years at the public personas created for them by the press and at what they believed were inaccuracies about the events surrounding their lives. The decision to publish her private writings was, consciously, her way of setting the record straight, and perhaps unconsciously, a way to satisfy a long-standing desire to be truly understood.

The "little girl who runs more slowly than the others," the one who is terrified of being left alone—that

Saint-Exupéry met through Anne's words in *Listen! the Wind*—is present in her diaries and letters, too. I don't know whether Anne ever truly "found" her and reassured her. But I know she tried. The longing to find this part of herself and comfort her is in everything she wrote.

In the last decade there have been a handful of biographies, one of which Anne authorized. When A. Scott Berg set out to do a biography on Charles Lindbergh and requested access to all his private papers, Anne graciously and unexpectedly granted him hers as well. "You can't write about Charles without writing about me,"[37] she wrote as she sent him the document that would open the door to all of her papers, including her remaining unpublished diaries and letters. In *Lindbergh*, Berg revealed an Anne whose devotion to her husband was just as strong as the Anne in the diaries and letters, but whose marriage was far more shadowed.

Anne's youngest daughter, Reeve Lindbergh, has illuminated Anne as well. The intimate portraits of her mother in her own published work, *The Names of the Mountains*, *Under a Wing*, and *No More Words: A Journal of My Mother Anne Morrow Lindbergh* have helped us to know her mother into her middle age and later years.

This work has added significantly where Anne's own story leaves off. We are left with an image of a complicated woman whose journey was both tragic and transcendent. This sensitive, aware, and gifted woman may not have ultimately overcome the feelings of self-doubt that lingered from her beginnings, but in her struggle to do so she left a remarkable body of work that lights the way for others. In the late 1970s Anne was invited to speak at her alma mater, Smith College. The title of her lecture revealed, perhaps, how she herself came to view her life and its significance. *The Journey Not the Arrival* may be the best way to understand her legacy.

Anne Morrow Lindbergh died on February 6, 2001. The words she wrote in 1944 when she learned of the death of Saint-Exupéry are true once again. For, like him, she was "...a sun or a moon or stars which light earth, which make the whole world and life more beautiful. Now the earth is unlit and is no longer so beautiful."[38]

With Anne's death, a light has gone out. But fortunately she didn't leave us bereft. Through her literary work the beauty and gifts from her spirit will shine on.

Bibliography

Lindbergh, Anne Morrow. *North to the Orient* (New York: Harcourt, Brace and Co., 1935)

_____. *Listen! the Wind* (New York: Harcourt, Brace and Co., 1938)

_____. *The Wave of the Future* (New York: Harcourt, Brace and Co., 1940)

_____. *The Steep Ascent* (New York: Harcourt, Brace and Co., 1944)

_____. *Gift From the Sea* (New York: Pantheon Books Inc., 1955)

_____. *The Unicorn and Other Poems* (New York: Pantheon Books Inc., 1956)

_____. *Dearly Beloved* (New York: Harcourt, Brace and World, Inc., 1962)

_____. *Earth Shine* (New York: Harcourt, Brace and World, Inc., 1966)

_____. *Bring Me A Unicorn* (New York: Harcourt Brace Jovanovich, 1971)

_____. *Hour of Gold, Hour of Lead* (New York: Harcourt Brace Jovanovich, 1973)

_____. *Locked Rooms and Open Doors* (New York: Harcourt Brace Jovanovich, 1974)

_____. *The Flower and the Nettle* (New York: Harcourt Brace Jovanovich, 1976)

_____. *The Journey Not the Arrival* (New York: Harcourt Brace Jovanovich, 1978)

_____. *War Within and Without* (New York: Harcourt Brace Jovanovich, 1980)

Lindbergh, Reeve. *The Names of the Mountains* (New York: Simon and Schuster, 1992)

_____. *Under A Wing* (New York: Simon and Schuster, 1998)

_____. *No More Words: A Journal of My Mother Anne Morrow Lindbergh* (New York: Simon and Schuster, 2001)

Berg, A. Scott. *Lindbergh* (New York: G. P. Putnam's Sons, 1998)

Notes

1. Anne Morrow Lindbergh, *Gift From the Sea* (New York: Pantheon, 1955) p. 29.
2. Ibid. p. 57.
3. Ibid. p. 50.
4. Anne Morrow Lindbergh, *Bring Me a Unicorn* (New York: Harcourt Brace Jovanovich, Inc., 1971) p. 114.
5. Anne Morrow Lindbergh quoting Antoine de Saint-Exupéry, *War Within and Without* (New York: Harcourt, Brace, Jovanovich, 1980) pp. 20-21.
6. Reeve Lindbergh, *Under a Wing* (New York: Simon and Schuster, 1998), p. 166.
7. Anne Morrow Lindbergh, *Bring Me a Unicorn* (New York, Harcourt Brace and Jovanovich:1971) p. 99.
8. Ibid. p. 224.
9. Interview with Reeve Lindbergh, "Charles Lindbergh and Anne Morrow Lindbergh" A&E's *Biography*: April 2, 2000.
10. Anne Morrow Lindbergh, *The Flower and the Nettle* (New York: Harcourt Brace Jovanovich: 1976), p. 510.
11. Reeve Lindbergh, *The Names of the Mountains* (New York: Simon & Schuster: 1992) p. 101.
12. Reeve Lindbergh, interview in "The American Experience: Charles Lindbergh," PBS, 1990.
13. Anne Morrow Lindbergh, Bring Me a Unicorn (New York: Harcourt Brace Jovanovich; 1971), p. 99.

14 Anne Morrow Lindbergh, *Bring Me a Unicorn* (New York: Harcourt Brace Jovanovich, Inc.1971) p.155.

15 Anne Morrow Lindbergh, *The Steep Ascent* (New York: Harcourt Brace and Co: 1944) p. 60.

16 Anne Morrow Lindbergh, *The Flower and the Nettle* (New York: Harcourt Brace Jovanovich: 1976) p. 224.

17 Thornton Wilder, *Our Town* (New York: Scholastic Inc: 1990) III. 100.

18 Anne Morrow Lindbergh, *Bring Me a Unicorn* (New York: Harcourt Brace Jovanovich, Inc: 1971) p. 126.

19 Anne Morrow Lindbergh, *Dearly Beloved* (New York: Harcourt, Brace and World, Inc., 1962) p. 187.

20 Walker Percy, *Lost in the Cosmos: The Last Self-Help Book* (New York: Simon and Schuster, 1983), p.27.

21 Nora Ephron, *You've Got Mail* (Los Angeles, California: Warner Bros: 1998).

22 Anne Morrow Lindbergh, *Locked Rooms and Open Doors* (New York, Harcourt, Brace, Jovanovich: 1974) p. 231.

23 Anne Morrow Lindbergh, *Locked Rooms and Open Doors* (New York: Harcourt Brace and Jovanovich, 1974), p. 287.

24 Mark Reaves, Ph.D., Director of the Claremont Career Center, Claremont, California.

25 Rainer Maria Rilke, *Letters to A Young Poet*, trans. by Stephen Mitchell (New York: Random House, 1984) pp. 23-24.

26 Ibid.

27 Anne Morrow Lindbergh, *War Within and Without* (New York: Harcourt Brace and Jovanovich, 1980) p. 143.

28   Ibid. p. 148.

29   Anne Morrow Lindbergh, *Dearly Beloved* (New York: Harcourt, Brace and World, Inc., 1962) p. 187.

30   Anne Morrow Lindbergh, *Dearly Beloved* (New York: Harcourt Brace and World, Inc., 1962), pp. 150-151.

31   Anne Morrow Lindbergh, *Locked Rooms and Open Doors* (New York: Harcourt, Brace, Jovanovich, 1974) p. 275.

32   Anne Morrow Lindbergh, *War Within and Without* (New York: Harcourt, Brace and World, Inc., 1980) p. 449.

33   Anne Morrow Lindbergh, *Hour of Gold, Hour of Lead* (New York: Harcourt, Brace, Jovanovich, 1973) p. 305.

34   Anne Morrow Lindbergh, quoting Laurens Van der Post. *Hour of Gold, Hour of Lead* (New York: Harcourt, Brace, Jovanovich: 1973) p. 214.

35   Anne Morrow Lindbergh, *The Flower and the Nettle* (New York: Harcourt, Brace, Jovanovich, 1976) p. 455.

36   Anne Morrow Lindbergh, *War Within and Without* (New York: Harcourt, Brace, Jovanovich, 1980) p. 98.

37   A. Scott Berg, *Lindbergh.* (New York: G. P. Putnam's Sons, 1998) p. 565.

38   Anne Morrow Lindbergh, *War Within and Without* (New York: Harcourt, Brace, Jovanovich, 1980) p. 447.

39   Elizabeth Berg, *Escaping into the Open* (New York: Harper Collins, 1999).

Acknowledgments

When a book has had a gestation period as long as this one, there are many people to acknowledge with profound gratitude. Some may be unaware that they have had any impact on the journey toward completion, but even seemingly insignificant or unrealized contributions have a way of fueling the fire and keeping a writer going.

I will always be grateful to Frank Rogers for first suggesting that I turn my passion for Anne Morrow Lindbergh into a writing project and for his book-collecting zeal. The support and encouragement of friends from my Princeton days spurred me to believe there was something to this interest of mine that I ought to pursue. Thank you for recognizing the spark: Steve and Laurel Harrison, Anne Borbely, Thaisa Farrar, Patricia Reilly, Susan Teegen Case, Danny Reese, and especially Carol Cook, whose steady friendship and support have transcended geography. Special thanks to Dan and Cindy Miller and Holly Bridges for helping me find my way to my editor Roy M. Carlisle. I am also indebted to my former professor, the late Dr. James Loder, who understood the importance of the inner life not only academically, but encouraged me to get on with understanding my own.

The friendship, love, and support of my St. Louis friends has sustained me over the long haul. Cathy and Bob Westwood, Christine Blair, Ceci and Steve Paul, Fran Werner, Peg Tichacek, and Cheryl Wolfe have been there for me since adolescence. I am grateful for their presence in life, death, and other important things, like trips to White Castle and Ted Drewes.

Thanks to my friend Zaki Mustafa, who was just a phone call away for any computer question or crisis that emerged. His technical expertise and exhaustive patience are a wonder.

David Rensin and Karen Jo Torjesen read early drafts of the book and offered helpful feedback. I thank them both for their kindness and astute advice.

Special appreciation is due to all those who graciously permitted me to include them in my reflections: Sharon Algozer, Janet Brooking, Carol Cook, Jean Dickson, Craig Dickson, Steve and Laurel Harrison, Beverly Jones, Georgenia Irwin, Frank Rogers, Justin Rogers, Cheryl Wolfe, and Marvin Wolfe.

Reeve Lindbergh's warm and enthusiastic response—first, to my idea for this book and later, to the book itself—has meant the world to me. Hers is a generous spirit.

I credit two people for having the greatest impact on the evolution of this book into its final form. Each held an unwavering belief in me and in this project that provided a touchstone from which I drew strength and courage along the way.

I am deeply grateful to Dr. Mark Reaves, clinical psychologist and director of the Claremont Career Center, whose compassionate presence and insight helped to facilitate my "escape into the open,"[39] enabling me to dare to make my dream a reality and write a more honest book than I would ever have thought possible.

Roy M. Carlisle, senior editor at Crossroad Carlisle Books, caught the vision for this book at our first meeting. Gifted editor that he is, he saw the book that was inside me and drew it forth. Along the bumpy road to publication, his resolve to see this project realized never faltered. I thank him for his insight, tenacity, sage editorial guidance, and friendship. In addition, I want to thank the entire team at The Crossroad Publishing Company for their enthusiasm and encouragement throughout the process of bringing Anne's insights to contemporary readers.

Finally, there is my son Justin Rogers, whose presence in my life is a gift. He is one of the most honest people I know, and he makes me laugh. I am infinitely grateful and proud to have him as a son. Yes, Justin, Lego proud.

About the Author

Kim Jocelyn Dickson grew up in St. Louis, Missouri, close to Lindbergh Boulevard. She graduated from Lindbergh High School (home of the Lindbergh Flyers) in the Lindbergh School District, and worked on the school yearbook, "The Spirit." She believes this immersion in all things Lindbergh may have predisposed her to a later interest in Anne Morrow Lindbergh, the wife of the famous flyer and hero, Charles Lindbergh. She came to realize Anne was a heroine herself.

Ms. Dickson graduated from the University of Missouri-Columbia *cum laude* and later earned an M.A. at Princeton Theological Seminary. As a seminary student she became intrigued with the writings of Anne Morrow Lindbergh. While fascinated by the public aspects of Lindbergh's celebrated life, what really interested her was Anne's inner life and spirituality. After unearthing a body of work that was largely out of print at that time, twenty years of study and research followed.

Today Dickson lives with her son in Southern California where she teaches and writes. *Gifts from the Spirit* is her first book.

OTHER TITLES OF INTEREST